TERRIAN JOURNALS'

ISSUING CITATIONS

(Thoughts in adventure taken out of context)

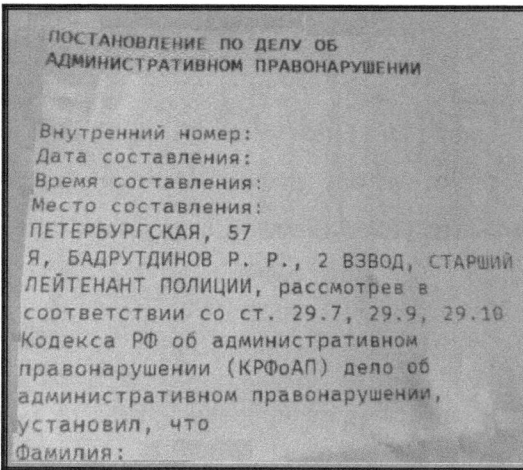

ПОСТАНОВЛЕНИЕ ПО ДЕЛУ ОБ
АДМИНИСТРАТИВНОМ ПРАВОНАРУШЕНИИ

Внутренний номер:
Дата составления:
Время составления:
Место составления:
ПЕТЕРБУРГСКАЯ, 57
Я, БАДРУТДИНОВ Р. Р., 2 ВЗВОД, СТАРШИЙ
ЛЕЙТЕНАНТ ПОЛИЦИИ, рассмотрев в
соответствии со ст. 29.7, 29.9, 29.10
Кодекса РФ об административном
правонарушении (КРФоАП) дело об
административном правонарушении,
установил, что
Фамилия:

by DONALD MURRAY ANDERSON

MSB

Terrian Journals' Issuing Citations

A Mythbreaker Book

First Edition

© Copyright 2024 by Donald Murray Anderson

ISBN 978-1-989593-44-8

For information address: mythbreaker@mail.com

(These citations are as startling as the Kazan traffic cop running to fine me about $C2 (reduced for early payment) for crossing an empty street on a holiday morning at a place without a traffic signal.)

The only certainty
is uncertainty.

The only insecurity
is security.

These writings surprise me as much as they do someone reading them for the first time.

How can anyone view anything in context without knowing the context itself?

Out of cite/Off cite

Composing this volume of <u>Terrian Journals</u> is a long process taking too many years.

It begins by searching for quotes in the first two sections of volumes of <u>Terrian Journals: Living As A Newcomer</u> when they are brand new.

Choosing cites becomes increasingly challenging.

Multiple volumes of <u>Terrian Journals</u> contain a plethora of cites, making the work of this volume limitless.

Here I order and expand the cites, but without changing their intent or meaning.

All the citations are quote-worthy, but readers need to proceed with great caution.

Herein is not a collection of inoffensive, comforting platitudes to relieve the stresses and disappointments of unfulfilling Sisyphus standard issue existence, while sitting on a chaisse-longue or a pedestal toilet.

The citations in this volume are unconventional, demanding, thought-provoking, challenging, and often absolutely annoying.

They reveal, expose, and defy conventional assumptions and mythical concepts of life that all too often remain unquestioned and unspoken because that would demand a complete rethinking and reconstruction of everything conceivable.

In the present volume, there are no holds barred and nothing is held back in a thoughtful and positive quest to make statements designed to bring about well-thought-out improvements to every aspect of thinking and of life itself.

These improvements are being held back and retarded by too many routine assumptions and notions "understood by all".

When "Everyone knows" everything, it is a barrier to human progress based on productive thinking.

In this volume, the background consenses which are invisible and expressed without thinking in daily words and actions cannot escape scrutiny and harsh criticism.

Each quote in <u>Terrian Journals' Issuing Citations</u> comes from a specific context of place and circumstance in the midst of human interaction and activity.

Each quote is inspired by actual events as they happen all around the writer, not rewrites after "sober second thoughts" or worrying about the actually thoughtless reality of what "people will think".

What is actually worrying is what people won't think and that they won't think at all.

It's also important to keep in mind that the contexts of <u>Terrian Journals' Issuing Citations</u> are non-temporal.

Time isn't as important as context if a citation is well considered, i.e. timeless. From the specific comes the general? Perhaps.

Quoting the words in this volume out of their non-temporal contexts can end up being inappropriate in the sense of interpretation and misinterpretation.

Almost any placid collection of quotations can be cited and is cited to support or justify completely different and opposite actions and arguments.

Take the satirical sketch about a nuclear power plant disaster caused when the last words of a retiring plant manager to his colleagues is, "You can never put too much water in a nuclear plant." (A line of dialogue in a skit featuring U.S. actor Edward Asner in an episode of Canadian Lorne Michaels' satirical comedy broadcast "Saturday Night Live".)

This type of ripe for misunderstanding quote can partially explain lavish praise and harsh critiques of an author's actual and identical words.

Ignorance quoting knowledge remains ignorance.

Some of the ignorance of quoting others to support a point of view is based entirely upon not truly knowing the author, her/his life, and his/her actual intentions.

Some of the ignorance is also rooted in merely following one of several common consenses and interpretations about the author as if they were absolutely true.

It's a <u>Cole's Notes</u> approach that almost ensures an English literature student a decent mark from an ingenuous teacher who says, "I want to know <u>your</u> interpretation, not one you read in a book. There is no wrong answer."

Yet the imaginative and different interpretation turns out to be "wrong" and evaluated as such.

Author Archie E(?) Anderson confronts this dubious practice of "teaching" by saying that he believes authors simply mean what they write. He does.

Authors are not usually writing secret codes to decipher and break like the ones Archie sends and receives during his youth in years of war.

In this spirit, to understand the quotes cited in <u>Terrian Journals' Issuing Citations</u>, it is only necessary to read <u>Terrian Journals</u> volumes in their entirety to understand the contexts in which the quotes are written. It's no secret.

I try to restrict my use of obtuse and double-entendre, triple entendre or more prose to humour writing. Outside that context, I try to write in a starkly direct way.

My citations have none of the couching and vaguery which I always believe is essential in academic writing intended only for the eyes of the professing, those who talk among themselves and hold absolute power over all who aspire to graduate.

Best to give them a better-than-mediocre impression than to attempt to be a daringly original non-graduate.

My citations have none of the politesse or kid-gloving of social gathering banter or idle chatter to "make friends and influence people" on the couch.

That's purely self-denial which primarily influences only the cautiously sociable. Everyone loves the boringly inoffensive, at least superficially.

The citations here are also not the endless rantings and sloganry of reactionary demagogue political candidates who are trying to please "everybody" and numb them into blind submission "followers" by shock and awe.

If there is a shocking reaction to my citations, it's rooted in the reader's mind, not mine.

Much of what I write is obvious from direct observation and careful thought.

The waves going through the mind are already a tsunami. The boat is already submerged. The apple cart is already tipped and toppling.

I'm only pointing out what's already in plain sight, yet unseen.

So why might some who know my observations and thoughts find them very strange? Why would they flee from them?

It's easier not to see and not to think?

It's easier to pretend that "everything is all right and will turn out fine" in "the best of all possible worlds", without giving it even a first thought and without making any effort at all to help improve anything?

That's "the way we've always done things". "Our best days are yet to come." We never have to change or take decisive action. (COPing mechanism?)

We are perfect and forever blessed, the best and the greatest of all? "Like" us. "Follow" us. Trust us.

No thanks. Not me.

Seeing The Cites

FIRST CITINGS
(preliminary sentences)

This is a collection of thoughts inspired by many adventures, places, and years of exploring, discovering, and thinking.

Together, the perceptions displayed in this writing reveal the impacts of one mind's eventful and thoughtful crossings of time and space.

This is the first volume of citations originating in the Terrian Journals series. There might be more to come. (Don't quote me on that.)

The citations are here presented all together under topic headings instead of as they actually arise in different contexts, which might create altogether unintended consequences for a reader.

Quoting out of context can reduce thoughts to disjointed abstractions and distort their meaning.

Knowing the contexts requires a thorough and careful reading of the original Terrian Journals volumes of writing in their entirety.

The mind telling of living as a newcomer, of thoughts in adventure is only highlighted in Terrian Journals' Issuing Citations. It's a preview, a teaser, and an incitement to read more.

Terrian Journals is an exploration of how we can realize ourselves as a living endangered species.

It's about recognizing and dealing with confinements which are handicapping us and hampering the process of fulfilling the potentials of our lives and our species.

Forewarning:

This writing is a call to action, not a tranquilizer or a pain killer to isolate, insulate, and prolong ignorance of the "outside world".

What you have before you is not a random collection of bland, unthreatening, polite, comforting, inspirational quotations and platitudes for religious-like meditations or for killing precious moments of a lifetime while using a toilet for a long time due to poor choices in diet and lifestyle.

The words and phrases here are not akin to a lively conversation piece for endless, idle hours of polite small talk and chatter to fill the empty hours lost to sedentary inactivity and unprogressive busy-ness.

This is not an ornate or pretty little booklet to put on a lounge table for leisure time recreation, something to casually ponder quietly from time to time in a comfortable arm chair as a source of abstract escapism, calm relaxation, and reassuring satisfaction.

The words in this volume will provide no sedative effect and will evoke no daydreams preparing the reader for an afternoon siesta or a lifelong nap from reality.

The origins and purpose of the writing in this volume are to promote healthy, fulfilling, positive, informed thinking followed by decisive action, to produce alternatives to being lulled to sleep for a lifetime or until species extinction overcomes us all.

This writing comes out of observation and action in reality, not from theoretical, isolated, indifferent contemplation and reflection conjured up at a secluded location.

This is writing to help awaken people from the suspended animation of routine, sedentary existence comatose, Sisyphus standard issue existence, and to get people on their feet, to stimulate minds to action,

This volume is no less than challenging and provocative, if not bold and action-inspiring.

It gives readers no opportunity to turn off their minds and to float into a "life is but a dream" world void, drifting merrily, eternally, and aimlessly in an out-of-mind experience leading to a happy blissful abyss of ignorance, paralysis, impotence, inactivity, and extinction.

The goal of this writing is not to send readers blissfully away to float in the clouds of some extra-worldly, heavenly Nirvana, where "a better place" is a solemn dream meant to be perpetually unattainable and unattained, except through death.

In what living mind can the goal and pinnacle of life be death? A deluded, hallucinogenically-altered mind?

For such a mind, if Nirvana ever comes alive, it can only be the work of "future generations" who will continue to only talk, in glowing terms, about "future generations" who will improve the world.

The result is a never-improving world, a product of eternal, generational procrastination. They'll do it, so I don't have to do anything.

I could try very hard to solve all of the world's problems, **BUT**... So I won't bother trying.

In reality, every "rebellious" and "promising" generation of "young people" ages and dies without reaching anything.

In sum, the thoughts in <u>Terrian Journals' Issuing Citations</u> are not intended to reinforce and encourage an escapist, isolationist, self-satisfying, self-congratulating, self-obsessing, perpetually-domineering, forever procrastinating, superiority-complexed mind set.

That fatal mental condition can only postpone a better world forever.

That fatal mental condition means only and merely pursuing the agenda and self-fulfilling prophesy of a forever acculturating "one world culture" with dilettante interventionism, temper tantrum punitive revenge, self-centred plaything obsessions, extremely xenophobic paranoid "security" defensiveness, violent aggression, and other destructive tendencies and characteristics that are typical of the behaviour of the "developed" or "first" world and all nation-states.

In such tendencies and characteristics lie the roots of the fall of all previous world orders imposed and enforced by monarchical dictatorship empires and their nation-state empire heirs.

If we don't change and eradicate these tendencies and characteristics, the hard work of making the world a better place will go to the people running the next world order that will soon replace ours as our aging, declining population falls into senility and dementia.

If the next world order is as dormant as ours, humanity will continue to repeat the same errors indefinitely, i.e., in Buddhist terms, humans will be trapped in an endless cycle of rebirths going backward into its primordial slimy origins.

24

We need to take decisive personal action before it's too late. We need to get moving instead of waiting to die in the comfortable fixed patterns and rutways ironically called a "way of life".

In fact, they are a way of existence producing only death, demise, and no tomorrow.

It's up to each of us to give ourselves freedom and opportunity, instead of giving up on ourselves and giving away our lives.

If more people become more Terrian-like, seeing human animals as an equal, not a superior member of Earth's living things which are sharing the same common homeland, the entire planet, there's more likelihood that there'll be more learning, more positive decisive action, and less idle procrastinating and perpetuating.

There'll be less inertia coming from deadly routines, conventional behaviours, and myths that are pushing us further along to our demise as the species that we call human beings, an increasingly fragile Earth animal.

There can be less inertia pushing us all further along to our unnatural end, i.e. completely eliminating our natural instincts, behaviours, and mobility.

Cosmological Context

While I'm exploring the very crowded, gigantic city of Rio de Janeiro for the first time, a Brazilian scientist discovers that the universe is limitless.

Why should the depth of a lifetime be any different or less natural than our larger than enormous home?

We need not accept limits, the very opposite of nature's limitless reality.

We need not limit ourselves to being the captives of societies, or organizations, or technologies, or nation-states.

We are by nature not dependents or slaves of the illusion called security.

We are an intelligence capable of surviving and flourishing.

We are energy and matter; we can neither be created nor destroyed. We just change form.

We are only short-term visitors on this planet. Let's see all of it and make the most of it.

Each precious day of life merits expression of what we would say if there were not another day.

The mythology of European astrologers confine the stars and planets to simplistic fixed shapes and constellations whose supposed movements and changing juxtapositions inalterably dictate individual character and destiny from the moment of birth.

It is the cosmological way of discriminating, stereotyping, restricting, and labelling people, affixing and fixating them into predestined, unalterable place for entire lifetimes, merely due to their purely random, accidental, and coincidental moments of birth.

East Asian astronomers see intricate kanji writing and castles in outer space. The universe can be read and interpreted in more than one way. Outer space is as an unlimited model for inner space.

What is the point of a great capacity computer, human or not, or a light-speed spacecraft, if they contain only elite memories and non-elite fossilized non-communication patterns?

Humanity's contribution to the universe should be more than trite elite/non-elite refuse, i.e. space junk.

If the star we call "the" sun were to explode today, Pioneer X and a few others would carry our ultimate message.

Each day an intelligent being has an opportunity to launch an ultimate message.

Each additional day of life is a day to improve upon the message.

Every day is a day to manifest intelligence.

Closeness to our nature is the opposite of fence-building and cosmetic gardening. We need wide open fields of food and beautiful growth.

Looking at the long, pointed church steeples, I wonder if future archaeologists might speculate that steeples are part of a space rocket religionism or a missile-fearing religionism.

Religionists' afterlife has little to offer me.

It's "heavenly paradise" means the boredom and annoyance of spending forever with a range of "fundamentalists" of various hues.

It's "hades" means the infernal annoyance of co-existing with those who cannot understand how anyone can live without alcohol, nicotine, caffeine, beef, possessions, and other drugs.

So my only hope is being alive, to the maximum extent possible and an eternity in limbo.

True adventure

True adventure has no when, except now; no how, except by any means and by all means; and no exactly where, except wherever the trails that we make, choose, and discover for ourselves take us.

Discovering the unfamiliar, whether it's a place, a person, a way of doing things, or even ourselves, might not be without hardship at first.

But learning how to overcome hardships is a natural part of being alive. It is part of our species survival instincts.

It's part of the challenge and the fun of living.

Geographic mobility means finding one's own way in life instead of being a captive or a follower.

Adventures don't run on schedule, or to deadline. That's why adventure is interesting, fun, revealing, and informative.

If people aren't limiting themselves and undermining their species survival instincts, by perpetuating the comfortable routines of permanent housing, motor vehicles, other possessions, and overly-dependent children, then we're already benefiting from exploring the unfamiliar together.

The moment that we let our artifacts, insecurities, and fears control us, we're giving up the central part of our humanity, i.e. control over ourselves and our directions.

We won't gain self-determination so long as we're only having a life adventure experience surreptitiously, in a pale simulation called "vacation", by fantasizing about "some day", by staring mindlessly at a screen, or by merely reading <u>Terrian Journals</u>.

Sedentary audiences of fiction, sports, and other entertainment, including Star Trek, are idly consuming adventure substitutes, placebos replacing real life in the "first" world.

The idea of space travel and the ideas expressed by the travellers excite the mind made dormant by unfulfilling routines.

Humanity is quite adept at finding, discovering, and inventing.

We only need to start giving ourselves the real freedom and opportunity to try to fulfill our common humanity.

Cut the weight; look at all the alternatives; maximize nutrition more simply and economically; and share all. Those are the adventure skills we have to learn.

Seeking beyond the limits, to the apparent ends of Earth, and then beyond, we set off to explore the wonders of the planet.

Would it be easier to stay "home" and forget about moving? Go to school. Go to work. Make money. Find a mate. Make babies. Get a mortgage and car payment plan. Get old. Die.

"That's life." Forget about fulfillment and adventure. Stay in front of the dulling light of the viewscreens. You can be "connected" without moving a nanometre. You are an appliance.

It is central to our being to constantly look for the point of interest just beyond viewing clearly. We never need a rationale or explanation.

We seek to seek.

Those who attempt to delay or to stop us are those who want to be our masters and to take control of our lives.

They want us to be employeed, citizened, and customered instead of learners, researchers, critical thinkers, readers, and writers.

In this adventure we are surrounded by learning opportunities.

If we make use of them, we'll be fully activating that human intelligence which improves our life-form's state for eons.

I mean before our current near-suffocation in dysfunctional societies.

We can learn how to live without slavery and serfdom again, and in this way open pathways light years long.

One thing to learn from adventure is that life is more challenging without employers and professors running our lives.

We have to be responsible, i.e. we have to be able to respond to anything and anyone entirely on our own.

We have to be responsible for planning our time to serve our interests.

As employeed and students, our days are dictated by people who only care how we serve them. Our time, lives, and thoughts are irrelevant to them.

Under them, we only need to mindlessly follow orders and instructions, primarily and almost exclusively for their general prosperity.

We are irrelevant zombies to them, resources to exploit with societies' license.

However, in adventure we must know what we want each day and act accordingly. No one acts for us. We take full responsibility for ourselves.

The new knowledge I gain in adventure serves me well as I live further beyond boundaries and horizons, contexts forbidden in conventional standard issue existence.

Every adventurer must return to tell the tale.

Patagonia, Inuvik, southeastern Asia, and even the Orly bomber(s) have been no obstacle to my adventures.

An adventure isn't a day at the amusement park.

It's not going through a fun house that's surprising everyone, the first time.

It's not going round and round in circles for a fast thrill on a roller coaster's fixed track or a slow ride on an anchored merry-go-round, or a twirl on a going nowhere Ferris wheel.

Adventure is going far beyond the rails and anchors, and not knowing exactly where we're going to land next.

Being indecisive can have very positive outcomes and reveal wonders.

Indecision planning seems contradictory but it means we don't choose one thing over another and we don't limit ourselves to only one.

We simply choose which to do first, with the order always changing.

I prefer to choose my own path, make my own discoveries, learn for myself about places and people first-hand, rather than through a filter of someone else's eyes.

I prefer to use my own innate ability to observe, judge, and decide for myself.

I tell no one my plans or my next moves. No one knows except me, and sometimes I don't even tell myself.

Adventurer says – No one knows all my plans and moves, including me.

I refuse to have someone else tell my fortune because I still make my own.

I don't know where I'm going, how to get there, or where I am. So every day is an adventure and life is always a discovery. It's fun too, unlike routine.

On a typical day I set out to go to one of two places, but end up somewhere else entirely.

In my adventures I seem to be like a Buddhist who, trying to get to Nirvana sooner, decides to live all lives at once instead of each life separately and consecutively.

One lifetime is not enough for me. I'm thinking about the sense of urgency that I feel about living.

The adventure trail can change like a breeze.

I could try to establish where I am by sending a post card to somewhere else, then looking at the post mark when I get there, if I ever do arrive there.

(There may still be unread mail waiting for me in Bolivia.)

But the post office here is closed today. Would I seem crazy if I asked a local, "What do you call this place?"

Ever time I set out to go somewhere, I end up in the opposite direction. My world is Isla Paquetá and Venezia.

Returning is a way of knowing where we have really been, where we are, and where we are going.

I go to Venezia from Chuang Hwa, to discover Marco Polo.

Knowing real adventure, I find holiday-like travel very superficial and unsatisfying.

Adventurous Terrian living is expanding my personal freedom.

When a person is worried or afraid of going to unknown milieux, it's time to get out and dive into the unknown.

It is better to have a lifetime and world of wandering and wondering than a lifetime of worrying in ignorance. There is so much to perceive that is imperceptible.

Hitch-hiking is challenging the unknown, never knowing who, when, what, where, why, or how until someone notices you, takes a closer look, and unexpectedly stops.

Someone and you take each other where neither of you can expect to be going, geographically and/or in your minds.

Long voyages at sea make room for inspirations, as the chains and anchors holding down the mind are cut from their moorings.

Being cut adrift lets me swim in the currents of thoughts.

The story of a voyage with no set itinerary and no final point is not only an adventure of a life time, it is a lifetime.

What is the optimum length of stay anywhere? It depends on the potential of learning compared with somewhere else.

The only way to evaluate the potential learning of one place is to move on to another place. A return visit might be possible, if promising.

People whose existence lacks adventure are deprived and wanting.

It is better for adventurers to make their own futures, rather than putting themselves in idler hands.

My adventures are natural behaviour.

The degree to which they seem extraordinary is a matter of the confines within which the reader places her/his mind and perspectives.

If I were less adventurous, I would feel as if I were crossing the legendary Japanese and Greek streams to a changeless afterlife paradise/purgatory, a milieu hardly worth experiencing at all.

Earth, "the world" is getting bigger for me each time that I become interested in exploring a different spot along its 40,000 km. rim.

It's only 40,000 km!

Illusion of Movement

Interhuman communication, encounters, visits, etc. are authentic. But, tourism is different. It's none of the above.

Tourism is entirely myth, with too many contrivances of intermediaries, manipulators, propagandists, and profiteers.

The dream vacation is much dreamier for the tourist industry than for the tourists.

Perhaps the rule of bureaucracy explains why people living in the intermediate latitudes are prone to turn to tourism for satisfaction or as a solution to their problems.

It's truly an escape from the unreal to the unreal by the unreal.

As a member of a tour group we become bit players, extras without lines in a plotless story.

We are as obedient and as expendable as foot soldiers who literally fall into line, stay close together, say nothing, and perish as unknown.

We follow, stay behind lines, remain silent, and act only on cue.

For peak vacation times, unfamiliar land is paved over and townsfolk are turned into circus animals or hucksters to entertain and bamboozle visitors.

Tourism turns productive people into sellers who wait for their incomes to be delivered by tourists who call sellers ignorant, greedy, lazy parasites.

Tourist slogan: Don't forget to wear your flag and be back in time for the commuter train.

European-faced tourists say, "The locals are slow and dishonest. They're like children."

I hear this insult around the world, always reserved for only non-European-faced and non-"first" world residents. Just a coincidence?

I see more slowness and dishonesty where I come from and in similar places of the European-face "first" world.

Why haven't the malcontent abroad seen that too? Myopia? Selective non-vision?

Do they live abroad longer than in their homelands? Or have they yet to truly live in their homelands?

People looking for hospitality and human warmth would be best to forego Europe and much of the "first" world.

Passports and visas are luxury goods that are available only to "first" worlders and to the elite "first" world* tourists of the "third" world.

(* not only "first-worlders living abroad, but including "first-worlder" elites native to the "third" world.)

All non-elite residents of the "third" world need not apply.

The tourist industry spends a fortune flooding the "third" world with inappropriate alien outside structures for superficial visitors who can have no more than a fleeting voyeur experience.

Only the "first" world and the elite "first" world of the "third" world gain from the lavish spending.

Tourist agencies are more dangerous than all the spy agencies put together. Tourist agents are the new crusaders, conquistadores, and missionaries.

They are "out there" converting productive people into servants of the "first" world elite. Locals become chamber maids, buss "boys", table servers, desk clerks, etc. getting $1 to $3 per day.

Some locals are pushed further into devoting their lives to the tourism religionism, actually becoming fanatical exploiters and swindlers of "first" world suckers.

While tourism gives easy free passage and easily affordable visas to the "first" worlder few and entertains them as honoured guests, many who wish to immigrate from the "third" world status continue to be blocked and maligned as "migrants" at the "first" world borders.

When the "third" are permitted to enter the land of the "first", i.e. the minority rulers of the world, the "third" must clean houses, drive taxis, labour in agriculture, etc.

This is the special status reserved for the "third" world/class citizens abroad.

Volunteering instead of dilettante superficial tourism is a minimal significant act.

Hundreds of millions of people have such an abundance of disposable funds that it would cost them very little to donate a few days of their vacation to volunteering.

The tourism industry's more than ample megaprofits can pay the conscientious visitors' costs while they're volunteering.

Imagine the impact.

Tourism is a psychological reaction to non-human existence.

Tourists on temporary and short-term leave from employment can do nothing except pay more money for less than they have at home, and contribute to destroying local economies and the planetary life-support system, by financing the tourist industry.

Tourists are paying their employment earnings to their employers' elite tourist industry counterparts, who pay minimum wage and less to tourist industry employees and provide no benefits to them.

Tourism turns potentially educational human encounters into cash register exchanges.

Tourism profits from and encourages illiteracy, communicative incompetence, and ignorance.

Anyone who can read, write, listen to, and speak another language and who can understand other human cultures, threatens and destroys the bases of a package tour.

It's packaged in illusions and myths.

Tourist brochures, guide books, and websites tell tourists "everything" they need to know prior to departure.

They are the ultimate guided tour. Every day and movement can be booked and paid for in advance.

Conclusion: If you know the answers before you set out, then you never really leave. Why bother?

The spectre hanging over humanity is tourism.

For people who only want to gripe, a "tourist destination" and "working abroad" provide more excuses to complain.

The tourist industry makes knowing who to trust more difficult.

Luxury hotels are another barrier dividing people.

Barbed wire and "security" keep out the "riff raff", i.e. ordinary local people who tourists need to meet to learn about the realities of the "tourist spot".

People staying in luxury hotels, like those in backpacker hostels, could be anywhere and nowhere, without knowing it. Better to stay home.

The hotel is such an alien base, reinforcing a false sense of dream world.

At best, visitors release their suppressed real selves.

At worst, tourists behave badly toward others in the safety of distance and anonymity from their homelands.

Soccer "hooligans" aren't unique in bad behaviour.

The military and diplomats go everywhere but never leave home.

They miss everything and everyone they could know. They live nowhere beyond their doorsteps.

It's an occupational hazard that they don't perceive or think about when mocking and criticizing the locals for not behaving like people "back home".

Believing that your place of residence is the epitome of all wonders cripples the human species' needs to seek, explore, and learn.

Why bother to even visit elsewhere?

Your place of residence is perfect – no question, no debate, no need to look further.

If your place of residence is a heaven on earth, it makes human life elsewhere redundant.

It reduces striving for improvement to wasted effort and foolhardiness. The perfect is already perfect.

This concept of an earthly paradise is an example of a very sad living death, a meaningless existence.

The tourist industry merely reinforces ignorance, prejudice, inequalities, and privilege.

It tells people from "heaven on Earth" that "there's no place like home."

The tourist industry is by no means a service industry beyond serving up self-serving reinforcement for self-congratulatory ignorance.

The tourist industry sends only reinforcements abroad to serve its cause.

Tour groups isolate while only complete stranger tourists connect. Singles attract.

Tour groups are too preoccupied with intra-group communication and joking about everything and everyone "local", agreeing on gross generalizations based on a sharing of collective ignorance.

Tour groups are a spectacle for locals, inhibiting and intimidating locals from trying to talk or communicate with the unfamiliar faces of the visitor hordes.

On Earth, if a person runs in one direction fast enough and long enough, s/he more quickly ends up where s/he starts out, and does not want to be.

(This is also a warning for people in the eastern part of Europe with a blind admiration and love for all things west of them.)

The world is not by nature a theme park for dilettante tourists. The world is a place for real life, not simulated lives.

Returning to their starting point, tourists say their superficial trips are so tiring that they need a vacation to recover from the fatigue.

They get that vacation in the form of a daily programmed experience of routines. Thus tourism instills and reinforces a craving for immobility.

The more inconvenient, far away, and busy the superficial tourist trip, the more appealing routines and conventions seem.

It's ingenious. Tourism makes an unfulfilling existence seem desirable.

A world safe from tourism would encourage only thoughtful, respectful, careful, well-briefed, and language-trained visitors.

They would stay a few months to learn, not to buy souvenirs, isolate in hotels or hostels, and herd together in alien tour groups.

Mere sightseeing would not be on the itinerary.

Nor would socio-economic disruptions, destabilization, and acculturation of local people encountered and visited.

Nor would environmental destruction and endangering the planetary life-support system.

Thoughtful travel and contact would help to positively unite humanity instead of creating and forever reinforcing a destructive love-hate relationship between the visitors and the visited.

Migrations

My home is anywhere with oxygen, water, and life.

An immigrant is a person who chooses to move from its area of birth to another area, to spend the rest of its life being called a "foreigner" by people living in the place by only accident of birth.

No matter where I go, I don't have the sensation of being a "foreigner" because I'm not alien to humans or this planet. There are no "foreigners".

I spend time with people whose company I enjoy, regardless of the interrelationships that we may have that are only an accident of birth or a moment of sharing the same space.

I meet people who are paid to be "foreigners" in Nippon. The ones I meet don't need to practice or pretend. They are naturals.

Instead of adapting and learning from their days in Nippon, they constantly harp about what they don't like here because it's not like their place of birth.

They learn nothing.

They try to assimilate me into their negative myths and behaviours, but they always fail.

I insulate myself from them so that I won't be isolated from Nippon. It is a joy for me to be here.

Travel tires and provides little knowledge and insight. So I migrate instead.

My experiences remind me of science fiction stories such as "A City In The Stars" and "Logan's Run".

The lead characters live in "perfect" domed cities and the ultimate caretaker societies.

The myth of their closed and isolated worlds tell them that everywhere beyond the dome is inhospitable and hostile.

But they go beyond and find wonders and make discoveries which change their lives for the better, and which reveal their perfect cities and societies to be unpleasantly flawed; misleading; distorted screens and filters of precious reality; stagnant and stale illusions.

Geographic mobility means finding our own way, not being a pawn on the tourist map game board, or an internet game avatar, or an employeed born for the sole purpose of being used (employed).

Are settlers stragglers in human migration?

We are not meant to be statues, fixed in place for eternity and posterity.

Otherwise we would be set in concrete or anchored permanently in only one place.

We would not have limbs which insist that we always move and change our place as often as we wish.

My grandparents do not stick around the tiny towns where they are born and remain there for a lifetime, waiting for the undertakers to plant their corpses next to their ancestors.

They don't become elderly people who still know only their former classmates from childhood.

They go thousands of kilometres away and never return to live in their places of birth forever after.

"...you cannot be kept in captivity." – my Carioca friend writes in my birthday card.

The price of the illusions of national superiority, of being a kept person, of superficial material comfort, is too high for me.

I do not seek to live in captivity.

"Things as they are" is a perspective which is never beneficial to anyone except dictators of all varieties. I thrive on fluid situations, change, liberty.

To "live in interesting times" is not a curse to me or anyone else. Such eras keep us alert, thinking, spontaneous, and adapting to unexpected change.

Life is an open set, an open environment experiment, not something in a test tube or an incubator or a fixed itinerary.

We need to be rude and ask uncomfortable questions, take gravel roads, and look beyond familiar horizons.

Seizing Chances

Nowhere is safe for any form of life. Being alive is dangerous everywhere for all life. That reality keeps life alert and strengthens life.

Living in fear is not living.

There is no security. Pursuing security is futile and folly.

Taking personal risks instead of merely settling for what's being put in front of us, like animals in a zoo cage, enriches our experiences and our lives; fulfills ourselves much more as human animals.

A person never knows when its life may be in peril. So every moment counts.

If a person doesn't do anything in life because of insecurity and fear, it is best to spend a lifetime in an incubator, a crib, or a womb.

Don't get too excited about currency trading, and take advice about it with a grain of salt, which, by the way, goes from being money to being a cheap condiment contributing to heart disease.

Life Time Values

Live life to the fullest twice, by living two years at a time in a single year. Live twice as long in half the time. Who says you can only live once.

How is this possible? Straddle the wacky international date line which says that two days occur simultaneously every day.

The time to live a full life is all day and every day. None of those precious moments should be sold and lost. It's too risky.

The squandering of human life is blatantly and obviously unnecessary.

The squandering goes on only because of mindless conformity and reproduction of the familiar mediocrity called routine.

Trading a life for monetary gain, banal routine, conventions, patterns set by our predecessors, and idle entertainment isn't a fair exchange.

They are the slowest ways to develop human genius, so slow that genius won't develop in an entire human lifetime.

Having the objective of financial gain alone is a hollow life.

It's the opposite of getting the maximum value out of being alive for less than one hundred Earth orbits around the star called Sun.

What good is money if the person using it is broken, diluted, diminished, or effectively dead from the employee experience?

The sum total of a lifetime should be more than a pile of "gomi" to be taken to the street corner by the next generation of slaves.

I'm going for far more than mere fame, money, and prestige. I seek to make and direct my own life.

Eating, sleeping, and moving are biological, not commercial or bureaucratic.

64

People with more financial assets and higher incomes should pay extra fees for services, but they should also have to stand in long lines and wait their turn with all the other members of the democratic electorate.

People who have servants are living beyond their human needs, have too many possessions, and have too much space to live in.

They have a delusional superiority complex and are actually incompetent at keeping their own houses in order and incapable of enjoying doing things for themselves.

It is reassuring, not fatalistic, to know that no matter what we do or possess in a lifetime, we all end up the same at the end.

All people die equally, are equally dead. Thus life is the ultimate egalitarian democracy.

Even the moneyed can't buy their way out of this human reality.

They are no better off than starving and homeless people in the end; and must mix with everyone as dead corpses, despite the artificial tomb walls housing each rotting carcass.

So our only worth and wealth in our lifetime, our only real legacy to others, is the way that we behave toward them and how they, in turn treat others.

Every life is equal. Its only value is in behaviour.

If we spend our living days worrying about being overtaken by death, we are already dead.

Our nutrition must never come at the cost of others' starvation.

Our opulence, our luxury must never come at the cost of others' homelessness.

Our lives and daily tranquility must never come at the cost of others' lives and tranquility.

Unfortunately, "first" worlders existence, in every part of the world, does come at great cost to more than 80% of the world population.

Before the present era ends and comes crashing down on our "first" worlder heads, we must correct our behaviour in order to leave a legacy of value to all future humans, instead of a planet without life as we know it.

The only true heritage and inheritance gained by each new generation is the way that preceding generations treat the world around them.

Our time is short and our human debt is infinite.

Our morality is spent on arms, and in support for dictators, and in the usury that we apply against the dictators' victims to pay us for our complicity in the dictatorships, only so that we can buy toys and games for ourselves.

Sharing our lives with others means sharing every part of ourselves and all that we call "ours". Our sharing needs to be far beyond our isolated enclaves.

A worthwhile act or gift is anonymous. It does not require or demand thanks or gratitude. It stands on its own.

If we go through life with a negative attitude toward humanity and low expectations of ourselves and others, it becomes a resignation from living and a devout religionist belief that life is predestined to mediocrity and/or evil.

This outcome is predestined only by ourselves – not by others and not by our nature.

Negativity toward humanity, including ourselves, becomes a self-fulfilling, self-defeating prophesy of unpleasant outcomes.

That makes us less humane and enables us to accept or justify lower standards of behaviour and to consider bad behaviour a norm rather than an exception which can be reduced until it is eliminated altogether.

Or we come to conclude that we should eliminate ourselves.

It's difficult to be our true selves in the place where we are born and brought up.

That milieu never ceases to be an environment which was set up to form us rather than to let us grow our own ways.

I come to life many times after my birth. In Rio de Janeiro, I begin a period of living life more fully than ever before.

The experience is releasing and unleashing potentials and abilities that I hardly know I have before arriving in Rio.

There, my Carioca friend's initial positive attitude toward me leads me to relish and thrive on my life even more, more than I ever do before then.

I aim to continue this way of living as long as I can.

There is much still to do, regardless of nay-sayers, health, age, etc.

The only real limits are the ones that we do not realize or perceive because they will surprise us unexpectedly.

I have no interest in people's excuses for not living their own lives, eg. "because of my family, my sex, my nationality, my parents, my friends, my society, my job, my old age, my security, my obligations, my responsibilities..."

A truly responsible person uses his/her life, living it to its fullest. Each person is ultimately responsible for his/her life, it's direction, and it's outcome.

In Brasil I meet people who want to have adventures, but who say that they lack the courage.

In the Van Couverden-Victoria area of Columbia (Br.) I meet people who are afraid to express their wantings and who just try to discourage me, to frighten me, and to mock my interests/objectives.

I leave all the nay-sayers in my dust. The nay-sayers/negative-thinking people are wasting away/rusting out.

My dad always says, "It's better to burn out than to rust out."

I now live on my interest, i.e. human interest. I have no mortgage on my future, or boss on my present. I explore, discover, learn, and grow.

My life is not a prison without walls.

Life is a precious moment to be fulfilled with energy, not sacrificed or compromised.

My life is not raw material to be molded by conservatives and conventionalists.

Conservatives and conventionalists are people without their own true futures of active choice.

They reject all futures that divert from the past and that open up a plethora of futures to explore.

Why does choice and human progress frighten them so much?

They will never know their true selves and never know what they truly want to do.

They are people put in molds at birth, put there by well meaning or bad-intentioned people.

The mold is a continuation of the impoverished lives of forebears.

It is easier to leave a mold imposed by the bad-intentioned.

They have set out with the intent of restricting a person's life.   They are like life-threatening diseases.

So they can be fought relentlessly and by every possible means.

Being conservative is a characteristic of followers of all ideologies.

But if the conservative becomes the centre in life, then hopes and dreams will never be attempted or realized, always put off or cancelled permanently in caution or fear.

Prejudice is always a hard vice to break, a hard narcotic mind set to overcome.

But human life depends on our triumph over our extremely bad habit, prejudice.

We must kick the prejudice habit before it stomps us out as a lifeform. Prejudice is the most fatal addiction.

In Canada's public transit, the faces I see are sometimes distraught and worried-looking.

These poor people, I'm thinking. Why don't they shut down this society that leaves them looking this way?

These people are maintaining the infrastructure and global inequalities which enable me to learn and write, instead of being trapped here as an employee, a passenger in an existence in which the employers set the schedule.

Life is a limited time offer. Take it or end up buried alive in a standard issue existence Sysiphus coffin.

That coffin is requisitioned, ordered, and grossly overpriced by others who do everything at the expense of your life.

Why is life an offer that so many automatically and thoughtlessly refuse instead of setting it as their life default?

The common human interest is health, not ideology or other religionisms.

A deliberate Spartan lifestyle is a healthy approach to life in the "first" world that can enable the 80% of non-"first" world humanity to flourish.

It has to be a rational choice, not an imposed lifestyle to end the era of the greedy denying the needy.

It is rational because it enables people in the "first" world to avoid consequences such as harsh retribution and total species extinction.

If we observe, analyze, and choose futures that are based on the essentials of earth and all lifeforms, human and non-human, we need not create in ourselves the suffering and stress of trying to suit the false, blind prophets of mindless conformity to the abstract, the narrow confinements which are called conventions.

Conventions are for the conned and convents?

Conventions are a form of ingrained prejudice?

Prejudice is an energy-saving device, requiring neither observation skills, nor thinking and reflection, nor experience in being alive.

The primacy of safety, security, isolation, and affluence in warding off fear of the tough unknowns of the "outside world" become the ruling myths of the "first" world.

The primacy of safety, security, isolation, and affluence places boredom and insatiable appetite and greed at the highest level – as the ultimate good.

The myth of "first" world immortality and hence disillusion arise.

The facts are – We and our era are mortal. Time limits us all. There is no certainty or security. Nowhere is safe.

It is impossible to isolate ourselves from the world, none of which is "outside". Affluence of the few results in poverty for the many.

To live is to live, not something to waste in lifelong hibernation or hiding in deceptively safe-seeming places.

Those who go along wide, paved roads to the woods "to get away from it all" are the ultimate product of this society of hiding – a society of the hiding.

We hide from nature in the woods and in the jungles of totem and taboo – of culture, tradition, custom, and architecture.

And yet is it also a société cachée, a prison with invisible walls inhabited by the deaf, blind, and mute by choice.

These miserable poor-by-choice live in love with debt or opulence and confinement.

I gladly report that I do not belong to these zombie enclaves. I go beyond.

How pathetic it is that humans can feel sad about not belonging, all the while denying a common human spirit which needs to first seek, explore, and venture forth, not burrow into the ground that happens to be under us when we are born.

A life's course can be set by oneself, subject to alteration as events occur. If not, the course will be set entirely by others and events.

For life is like a journey on the seas. Skill in navigation and sailing means the strength to deal with waves, currents, and sudden storms.

I am a student, so I study. It is a statement of dedication to learning, which typifies anything that I do with volition and energy.

I am a writer, so I write.

A person's real work, as opposed to the servitude called employment, is what s/he does because it is of worth and importance to him/her.

It is, in itself, of value to her/him.

In natural human behaviour, it provides each person, directly, with the essentials of a lifetime, eg. physical and intellectual sustenance; motivation to act and reflect; a sense of direct contact with our selves and the environments, etc.

It is a planet far away from possessions, comforts, money, and "jobs".

It is nutrition and flourishing.

I just enjoy living, trying to do as much as I can, and seeing myself as constantly struggling with conventions and myths that conspire to trap us all and hold us all back from achieving our full human potentials.

A younger person should not be restrained by old games and old rules.

A younger person's life should not waste his/her most vital years and be held back by fame, fortune, possessions, or the pursuit of the illusion of security.

These are only hindrances on mobility and freedom for all of us of all ages. Holding back the youngest holds back us all.

The hindrances almost completely eliminate our ability to walk unnoticed and to thus observe and to learn unmolested, in the midst of humans going about their daily lives.

We must not be lured away from our lives by deadly illusions which can destroy our ability to enjoy being alive.

We must all run at maximum speed, to do what we wish with each precious instant.

We must look disconcertedly toward our nearest star, Sun, as if it were about to fizzle out and freeze us or to vaporize us as a super nova, before we can complete our true selves.

There is no fate, no destiny. Life is neutral. Coincidence and action are the stuff of living.

Territoriality and a lust for possessions come from the conditioning called "societies" & "economy of scarcity".

Routines replace being alive, like creatures taking over the world in "Invasion of The Body Snatchers" movies.

Life Struggles

A life is to live. This is the birthright of every living being. A life belongs to the one living it, not to other who are living other lives.

Taking another's life is not restricted to physical murder.

Hindering and preventing another from living a life to her/his full potential, as s/he defines it, is taking another's life.

A living human is obliged only to do as much as s/he can, no regrets. That's her/his only true responsibility in a lifetime.

Title is nonsense. We are all human beings – the only real title.

Names are forgotten and currency dissolves into dust.

Myths, illusions, conventions, routines, nation-states, and other artefacts are only running our lives because we're letting them do so.

Without us, without our passive compliance, they have no power over us, no meaning whatsoever in our lives.

They need us. We don't need them.

Some people make their jobs their lives. I make my life my work.

Retirement is all about theoretical future outcomes and incomes. It's about planning a harsher and bleaker reality.

Retirement is all that remains after a life is deforested, strip-mined, sapped, and completely depleted. There is no restoration plan.

Retirement schemes are just that, never intended to be thoughtful, comprehensive, and lasting. Schemers aren't long-term planners.

Pension funds, like insurance policies, are based on the statistical probability that not everyone will collect.

Of those people who do live long enough to collect pensions, few will live long enough to collect very much.

Pension plans risk their capital in stock markets which are less predictable than the longevity of pensioners.

A retirement poster should display an older person who's pointing at wrinkles, arthritis, and age-segregated institutions.

The caption would be: "I've been working all my life for this."

No matter how adventurous we're getting, sometimes it's hard to avoid taking the safest, most secure vehicle of the status quo traveller through at least some moments of a lifetime.

These are lost moments of life.

The mainland is less than two kilometres across the sea from Alcatraz Island.

The island guide is explaining that regular warm showers keep prisoners from trying to escape by swimming the short stretch of water to freedom.

The theory is that inmates getting two hot showers per week can't start developing a tolerance for cold water, which would condition their bodies for the cold sea water flowing between them and their freedom.

Unlike those prisoners, so many of us are giving ourselves warm showers all the time, holding ourselves back from swimming in the wider streams of life.

We're making ourselves far too comfortable for taking on challenging, fulfilling lives.

We're feeling too warm for leaving, exploring, progressing, creating, and developing.

We're drowning our species survival instincts and the skills we gain from all previous generations.

Our Alcatraz too is a training centre that's teaching us how to live the prisoner's life for a life sentence which we will pass on to all future generations.

We completely forget that it's the responsibility of every prisoner to try to attain freedom, not to escape challenges beyond the mundane, conventional walls.

"Maximum Security" is just a clever sign on a commercial building in downtown Montréal.

But it's making me think that people wanting to maximize security in their lives are ending up living in self-made prison cells.

Be it ever so short, a human life can be worthwhile.

How many healthy, "first" world dwellers can honestly say that they relish life and thrive on it during at least ten years of their prime, pre-aging, adult years of life?

How many don't just sit and casually stare at nothing while their lives go by, flashing before their eyes long before being declared officially dead?

Being alive means more than mindlessly doing what is expected. Being live means doing what is unexpected and unpredictable.

Being alive means carrying on along toward always unexpected futures and dealing with them in unpredictable ways.

Human genius

Few people are called geniuses because such great restrictions are imposed upon people by societies that anyone who succeeds in fully expressing him/herself looks like a genius.

...Every human being has genius. We just need the time and opportunity to develop it in our own way and at our own pace.

Genius is expressed by everyone who uses his/her natural intelligence instead of accepting things the way they are said to be by dulled minds.

Human progress comes from a widespread liberty of creativity and expression and the amount of room given to explorers, inventors, and artists of all types and varieties.

Unfortunately, in my schooling obedience, order, and continuity are the top priorities.

Cogency and coherence are taught, but free thinking and innovating are left to float aimlessly, until they sink forever out of view and drown.

During the very rare moments when creativity might appear in a schoolhouse, and might be tolerated, it's only an afterthought and labelled an oddity coming from a "dull" mind.

My schooling considers creative behaviour to be rare genius, confined to a very small number of people called geniuses who appear like magic, a miracle among humans.

The rest of us are all dull dolts and duds.

The rarity and minoritization of "genius" is evidence of the failure of the "education" system and the society behind it.

A television interviewer and a creator of artificial intelligence (AI) agree that AI will replace humans as the most intelligent lifeform on Earth.

Given the shortness of the human reign on this planet and that reign's extremely destructive behaviours since at least the "industrial revolution", why do the interviewer and creator believe that humans are the most intelligent form of life on Earth?

After about 40 million years of ruling Earth, dinosaurs are wiped out by a cosmic catastrophe that is well beyond their control.

Human animals wipe themselves out in a mere couple of hundred years, out of sheer stupidity. Humans are the ultimate "dumb animal".

Using technology to express intelligence has a major drawback. All electronic works can be eliminated in a moment when the technology fails.

Meanwhile, the cave drawings of our ancient "primitive" ancestors remain writ in stone.

The national pavilion of Shiite-ruled Iran, at the Tsukuba International Expo in Nippon, displays the scientific, mathematical, and other accomplishments of the ancient Persian civilization, not blind faith and obedience to absolute givens.

Adaptation Needs

We are becoming aliens on this planet, unable to nourish and house ourselves, unable to survive without the most elaborate protection and pre-cautions.

Will future humans wear space suits on Earth?

Human animals risk the same fate as other Terrian forms of life unable to survive the natural atmospheric-biological-gravitational conditions of Earth.

Environmental problems are inherent to anchored sedentary ways of living.

Everything around the anchor is despoiled, poisoned, paved over, and abolished, including life itself.

I'm living within the natural environment as best I can, and trying to raise my consciousness of it wherever I'm going.

Those who destroy the human life-support system of Earth, without giving it a first or second thought, must be either hostile alien invaders from somewhere else in the universe or represent a type of human which has lost all of its natural human animal survival instincts.

Humans who don't progress are like recording devices that are playing back the docile, intransigent, and routine behaviours of other generations.

If we remain in a milieux, we mirror it.

Thus, trans-social migration is necessary to enable us to differentiate among social, human, and individual characteristics.

When everything changes, the changers lead.

True Selves

When we're denying our true selves, we're becoming like trappers who set leg hold traps for ourselves, get caught in them, and then pretend they're not there.

We end up causing ourselves inexplicably needless and endless pain, while preventing ourselves from moving in any direction, anywhere at all.

Having power over one's own life means defining one's own reality, drawing one's own maps, writing one's own lexicon – not letting others do it for you.

We can cultivate the best in each, as defined by each, or be true to others instead of our own reality and being.

Unify what we are, what we think, and what we do.

Directing my own life is risky and difficult. But I accept any consequences, beneficial or otherwise.

I can do so because I have the overwhelmingly satisfying knowledge that:

i) The consequences are a product of my own thoughts and actions alone;
ii) I make it happen.
iii) I make my life and whatever it produces;
iv) I am my own purpose;
v) My life attempts to do what I will.

Scientific research on display at a Paris (France) museum ("Musée de l'Homme") shows that "racial" characteristics overlap "races".

There is no scientific basis for dividing humans into "races". There are no races. Race is only a myth that divides and hinders us all.

Our true selves must always resist and reject all attempts by the self-denying to force us to justify, defend, and deny our lives reflecting our true selves and to conclude that we should abandon our true selves just like the self-denying do.

A person who allows him/herself to think freely, to go beyond the definitions which societies try to impose upon him/her, can find in the world many people and places where and with whom s/he can live in harmony.

Not sexy

Life can be one-sided for anyone wanting something but hesitating to try for it entirely due to constant pressures not to try.

Generations of women and men lose their lives around the world, not through death but while still living and breathing.

This tragic and needless loss of life occurs because they solemnly, even if unconsciously believe that their lives are a fulfillment of only what others expect of them.

Too many women in too many societies are never meeting their full, individual, human potential because they're being brought up to believe that they have no future and no worth if they're not accepting restricted roles and status in relation to men.

...A husband may be just someone who's there to "have and hold" back a woman. He's "keeping" her like a zoo keeper. Stay in the cage and all is well.

It's difficult for me to establish a friendship with a woman who is so trapped in social roles that the first question she asks me is "Are you married?"

Having a "married" friend is taboo? It's only okay for same-sex couples to have opposite sex friends?

Women are given two choices in life. One is to remain slim, until pregnancy. The other is to become fat and thus not to attract airhead men who only evaluate women by weight. What choice?

To this very day, younger women are discouraged from eating full balanced meals to gain the physical and mental strength coming from good nutrition and the natural growth and development it supports.

Women with physical and mental strength threaten men lacking self-confidence.

Thus sports segregates people by sexual characeristics, regardless of physical strength and abilities, so that women won't be able to publicly embarrass under-confident men by out-performing them in sports.

Sports people undergoing sexual change procedures upset the whole notion of segregation based entirely upon gender.

Let all humans participate in all sports as equals based on strength and abilities, such as a desegregated form of heavy-weight boxing, instead of forcing people to limit themselves and their competitors merely due to sex.

Unrolling Humanity

Sexual inequality is <u>not</u> based on the longest-term historical facts of human life.

If females were naturally weak, feeble, meek, incompetent, stupid, and inferior, as obnoxious male fictions and frightened male dictatorships depict them, the human species would be a long extinct form of life.

Sexual inequality is a squandering of the human intelligence and potential of at least half the human population and thus severely retarding human progress as a whole.

Women are prevented from perceiving and knowing themselves as equal human beings.

Sexual inequality is thus a crime against all humanity.

Dividing a single atom creates a devastating explosion. Humanity is a single atom.

...All I'm trying to do is use my brain to make my own life. Nothing more, nothing less.

A person who wastes energy considering the harm or hurt that every thought or action could involve might end up spending an entire lifetime as a servant of all around.

This person is no longer alive.

Human minds and capacities are naturally capable of all functions, not just one.

To do each function exceptionally well, concentrate and perform each function in turn.

It's like studying each subject separately instead of the confusion of trying to study them all at the same moment.

It is absolute fantasy that a human being limit itself to only a single type of activity for the larger part of a lifetime.

That's like being a nationalist. It only provides a very narrow, restricted view of life.

A human being is a forever solitary creature, not merely a social animal. To say otherwise is an easily disproven myth and falsehood.

Birth* and death are singular experiences of one person at a time, not shared or shareable, even in a disaster or war's mass-killings.

(*In the case of birth, singular applies to the person born. The mother is not born giving birth, except in a social semantic sense.)

Twins and multiple births are not simultaneous shared experiences. There are gaps between each individual birth.

Only congenital siblings who are born together, physically joined, attached, and sharing vital organs can honestly say otherwise.

Learning occurs in each brain separately, not in a classroom, lecture hall, or other audience.

Each learning brain needs to be attentive and active, not drowsy, uninterested, or distracted.

Different natural human brains are located in different bodies, not physically connected.

It's a pity that humans regress so much from their nature that their nature itself becomes a mere commodity. A glaring example is the sex industry.

Another is the public toilet business of the European peninsula.

If food, shelter, water, and a free toilet aren't basic human rights, then what is?

To those we love, there are only a few words of value: "Do as you choose. That's what's best for you."

If they ask advice, we say: "Only you know yourself, but if you think I can offer any useful counsel, ask me specific questions. I can only try to tell you what my experience, not yours, has told me. My words are less likely to apply in your case."

These are honest, truthful ways of communication. No one is competent to decide another person's life.

If we do not respect the other person's self, we will find ourselves gradually excluded from it, as the self defends and protects itself from our assaults.

A self that does not set its own path can only perish, by self-denial or annihilation from outside. Each life is too precious to suffer this destruction.

If we constantly and continuously tell another person who s/he is, and s/he starts to believe us, then s/he and we will never know his/her true identity. Nor will s/he.

A life changes according to the information it both receives and uses.

Lock-step dancing makes me think of the robots' questions of my non-robot ways.

Your negative critical questioning of my behaviour and personal choices needs analysis, not my behaviour and personal choices.

What kind of a narrow society do you represent that causes you to question what you find different and thus uncomfortable, troubling, and challenging to your perspective?

Your perspective is derived from monotonous, unquestioning conformity, lock-step production line routine, duplication, repetition, and blind acceptance?

A martyr is a person who dies only because her/his personal choices and beliefs are adamantly opposed by others.

Instead of dying a martyr, it's better to live and to set a good example of what's possible.

Why do religions portray good behaviour as extraordinary, instead of ordinary like breathing?

Whether one lives 50 years or 100 isn't important. What matters is having done at least one thing which has been fulfilling for oneself in one's life.

Doing more than just one such thing is much better.

The study of history needs to be about finding out who we really are, where we really are, and how we really live. At present we still don't know.

Perceiving Inside Out
(the inside world)

Those touched by the horizonless horizon find boundaries unnatural.

It touches anyone who roams into the middle of prairie flatland; sails into the open Earth Ocean where no shorelines can be seen; and explores outer space.

Leaving routines, conventions, and other boundaries behind makes everything and anything conceivable and possible.

To know what one knows and does not know and to know what one thinks is to step outside of a time and space trap called society.

Stepping outside means trying to use your own eyes, ears, and all other senses, not your society's senseless conventions.

Discovering the illusions of another society through your own senses can enable you to perceive the illusions of your original society too.

Unfortunately, few do so. Instead they become harsh critics of the "outside world" and compare it unfavourably with their "perfect" original societies.

The way to accurately perceive what's always around us is not through the veils of conventions or the anxieties, expectations, myths, and misinterpretations of others, but through our own senses.

The way to perceive the world from distant, unfamiliar perspectives is more challenging.

...Looking at the world through someone else's eyes requires a lot of focusing.

Hearing the world through someone else's ears requires finely tuned listening skills.

Accurately perceiving the world through someone else's senses requires much more than empathy. It requires intensive and objective study.

Although I manage to deeply infiltrate the daily living experiences of various people in this hemisphere of the continent, I remain outside certain realities here.

Sometimes the door frames are less than 188cm high, so I have to remain outside. I try to duck.

The military dictatorship of the time is running a TV commercial showing demonstrations in the street before the coup d'état long before my arrival here.

A voice-over says that the country was in chaos. Then it says, "But thanks to the armed forces, order was restored."

Yes, 20 years of "order", of lost initiative, of no human progress, of mindless repetition of routine.

But this is not exceptional or exclusive to military dictatorship. It's just less subtle here than in places with indirect democracy elections.

How can military dictatorships ever be allies of democracy, and vice versa?

I try to see my living sites inside-out, not outside-in.

Heart Beat

Brasil's music is profoundly more alive and natural than the decaying artefacts called nation-states, religions, societies, etc., with their armies of bureaucrats and soldiers.

Brasil exists in spite of them.

Brasil is the melody of all humanity. Brasil is teaching us how to make harmonious sounds together.

Brasil is the centre of our humanity. It's the land of combining the whole human, shaping us into realizing that we are a single species, the human race.

Brasil is showing all humans an alternative to separating ourselves from ourselves into rigidly barricaded nation-states.

Brasil is showing us our common identity, instead of deceiving us into becoming self-denying predators who are only hunting ourselves down and killing only ourselves with self-inflicted wounds.

Video Void

Music on video, visuals over sound can confine or drown out imaginative listening and distract us from the sound appreciation of music.

Special effects and cinematography can make the songs into no more than sound tracks, peripheral instead of central.

It is video karaoke* with a voice-over.
(*correctly pronounced: car-ow-kay)

We are too confused by volume to think before we buy on impulse.

As a lifeform, we no longer create music?

Music becomes a specialty which only experts create, for the sole purpose of trying it out on human test animals to determine its effectiveness in eliciting the required response?

You can learn a lot more from gazing at a tree than watching a day of TV. Look at the scene, instead of just the screen.

In times past, the cathode ray gun is a debilitating weapon pointed at the passive, sedentary human and irradiating its brain.

Then the newer blue screens become far more hypnotic and entrancing, constantly and relentlessly demanding undivided attention, not just once-in-a-while or regularly scheduled tuning in and watching for an entertainment hit.

The result is concentrating more and more on less and less.

For years the blue screen rays sap youthful minds and faces, rendering them old beyond their years, leaving only artificially aged Rip Van Winkles who, if they ever do finally wake up, find themselves about to die.

In Tune

(lyrics of humanity)

It's time for reuniting humans with the rest of nature, turning on our combined power and knocking out the artificial circuits that are entangling and strangling our lives and our livelihoods.

The human sound in nature is music singing in harmony, echoing and responding warmly to the sounds of the natural environment.

Learning

My sole thirst is to learn about the planet and its life, especially human.

Learning to learn is a cerebral and physical activity, not an institutional structure or certification.

Movement enables more profound learning and more reflective communication than docile, sedentary lifestyles.

Sitting at a desk to receive a lecture is not profound learning. It is paralysis. Learning will go farther and further in a wheel chair. Quickly roll away!

I so often realize that my education is so lacking. I am so ignorant.

After all my years of "first" world schooling, I know almost nothing of the Americas and African pre-European cultures, civilizations, and histories.

Whose education is really deserving of the label "third" world, in the epithet sense?

Future historians may conclude that the inability of the schooling system to motivate, inspire, attract, and retain students voluntarily, without the employment threat, is part of the "first" world's undoing.

Without the high standards of education needed to attract and motivate students, the "first" divide against themselves, eg. Canada, and stall while the "third" world move forward.

There is often talk of "going back to the three 'r's", to find the road to the future. It's based on illiteracy since only reading begins with an "r".

Basically, an obsession with "three 'r"s" just keeps people going around in circles, instead of advancing in humanity.

Know what you know and what you don't know.

There'll always be much more you don't know than you'll ever know.

Expression

Direct, simple language is the road to communicating with the majority of people, who hold the controlling interest and votes in a democratic form of government.

The French Créole language is like the Latin Créoles, which became European languages, and the still formative Anglance languages, such as Japanese-English and Singlish.

The spread of the English language leads to its ultimate demise, as other language groups render it unrecognizable and incomprehensible to people who use English as their first and only mother tongue.

Who among the Europeans would have thought, during the empire of Rome, that Latin would not now be the "world" language?

I don't give anyone a piece of my mind, but all of it piece by piece and whole.

Both mediocre and ineffective English language education help to keep the world from being robbed of our rich human heritage and diversity.

Mediocre English language usage in journalism further protects our rich human languages heritage and diversity.

There is thus hope for the 6,000 human languages.

Less than 10% of the world population speaks English as a first language. As non-anglophone populations increase in number, the percentage declines.

Each non-anglophone elite adopting English changes it to local pronunciation, while altering word usage and grammar.

This foretells the birth of Anglance languages in a world where English, like Latin, isn't spoken by anyone.

Anglophones collaborate in this process by their ignorance and sloppiness in their first language.

Some anglomaniacs must see free trade with the U.S. as their last chance to try to reverse linguistic equality advances in Canada and to eradicate it's 100 languages.

I'm not English.   It's only a language I use to express myself.

I'm not English.   I only spent a few months in the English part of the U.K.

If I'm not Canadian, I must be Japanese.   I live in Japan for years.

One lesson to learn from Colon's logs:

Making observations and conclusions without knowing local languages is a precarious way of making discoveries anywhere.

It is looking at the world through only a colon.

I wonder what my thoughts could be avant of?

I write what I think, feel, see, etc. regardless of the conservative fad of the day.

Human rights egalitarianism and inner expression are not a mania for me. They are constants in my thinking.

It is in every human's best interest to foster multi-lingualism and multicultural consciousness in anglophones, instead of just creating deputy-elite anglophiles, who only say what the ignorant anglophone elite wants to hear, with cute or incomprehensible accents.

Only in a world where there is widespread respect for the value of many languages can the native speaker anglophone minority (less than 10% of the human population) hope to be permitted to retain its language after the imperial structures holding it up fall apart.

Learning English is merely an exercise in how to learn a language and many languages.

The prime goals of learning a language are not to pass a stilted artificial test; not to seek employment (including promotion and increases in financial income); not to go shopping; and not to become a tourist abroad.

The prime goals of learning a language are to increase and improve human understanding and to help us all to live together peacefully, harmoniously, and cordially.

This profound and highly productive intra-human communication can only come from learning each others' languages, not English.

The English language is borne of only one cultural group, those living in England, and their descendants abroad.

Communicating together does not mean abandoning our first languages and the cultures from which they are born.

English, like Latin, is used by domineering empires as a means of eliminating all other human languages and cultures, to reduce humanity to a characterless monolith; to melt us into a pot containing a colourless, bland, and tasteless human stew.

124

Omnipresent Isolation

Meeting and talking with a mariner and a trucker is a great opportunity to learn so much from people who are richer in experience and far more familiar with great expanses of Earth's land and sea surface than ourselves.

They can help most of humanity overcome the ignorance of an always-anchored-to-one-location existence.

Not learning from mariners and truckers makes most people more isolated than these long-term, world-knowing people.

Art demands active, not passive minds.   It demands an exposure to living reality, not an isolation chamber, padded cell existence.

Islanders tend to believe that their islands are more attractive than the outside world. Yet their island view is outside the world.

The island view can give residents and visitors a sense of being at the centre of the world.

The "outside world" is an alien certainty that the islanders may never know and never dare to know.

If they do go beyond their insular shores, their belief will soon be shattered, unless they leave their minds on the island.

All islanders do not live on bits of land surrounded by the waters of Earth Ocean or by fresh water.

The island exists anywhere and somewhere, but never beyond that one place, even if the islanders physically move as tourists somewhere else for a few days.

Ride Hikers

Every hitch-hiker standing at roadside could be an opportunity to know the unfamiliar, to meet and perhaps take a close look at a representative of a different world.

I'm willing to try living in a world where none of us would be anchoring ourselves, where we'd all be able to start living freely, instead of as captives.

We'd be exploring and discovering together, without hitching and without staying in fixed dwellings.

PRIME THREATS TO HUMAN LIFE:

1. Extraterrestrials:
Humanity's Broken Home

The prime goal of nation-states is to divide and conquer a single life form on one planet.

Nation-states rely upon building artificial boundaries with the sole intent of dividing humanity.

Nation-state barriers to human movement, intercourse, and understanding are completely unnatural and the essential first strike in initiating a perpetual human civil war.

We are one life form. (not nationals, not citizens, not congregations)

We are united by our humanity, intelligence, and imagination.

We are divided by constitutions, contracts, treaties, texts of all types, and other paperwork, in print or out of print.

2. Consenses of ignorance

Exotic places have exotic reputations, which turn out to be exotic compared with their realities.

All the information, from every source, that I have about the southern Americas before coming here, is turning out to be entirely false and misleading.

People living in Valdez (Alaska) a hundred years ago recount that demons & monsters live in the crevasses of Arctic glaciers.   (according to the museum at Valdez)

Before and after my visit, the demons and monsters reappear in the form of oil slicks and the petroleum companies pouring them over Earth Ocean.

Putting knowledge ahead of elitism is not "reverse snobbery". It's simply manifesting creative, informed intelligence.

3. Collective dementia

Tourists display severe symptoms of memory loss.

They forget their entire previous lives in their homelands when they go abroad to play, visit, work, live, or riot during "sporting" entertainment events.

With memory gone, taking civility with it, tourists become bit players with significant parts in producing a destructive tragedy for themselves and their hosts.

4. Worst people abroad

The worst people I meet live abroad, i.e. in the "first" world.

I meet them long before I start exploring and living outside my "first" world land of birth.

I'm not saying that all people there are bad, only a too memorable number of them.

5. Loss of life

If we lose our lives, if we lose our membership in humanity, we lose all that really matters.

Our sentimentality becomes misdirected into materialism and other illusions, instead of acting upon our global human interest and planetary needs.

We must not be lured away from our lives by deadly illusions which can destroy our ability to enjoy our lives.

Being satisfied is being dead. (AEA) There is nothing left to do or to look forward to doing.

To think and act on one's own is true responsibility, the ability to respond. Whatever happens in my life, I can take full credit or blame.

There is no room for self-underestimating or for complaining about and blaming others for my own choices.

In my ultimate manifestation of responsibility, I don't confuse possessions with needs or material wealth with a rich life.

In contrast, so many people use the self-effacing behaviours called employment and raising children as excuses for not accomplishing what they want to do and intend to do, and for not contributing to human or planetary interests.

Those are "respectable" excuses for doing nothing to contribute to human progress, i.e. irresponsibility.

By not parroting and mimicking those excuses, to a chorus response of "oh sure", "of course", and "wonderful", I leave myself open to charges of greed and self-interest.

But that's like accusing a non-nicotine-addict and non-pollution-vehicle owner of doing nothing to stop air-pollution.

Production and industrialization make human life more precarious and more difficult to support by removing access to resources for living.

Oxygen is converted into polluted air. A lifetime is converted into employeed subsistence existence. A close community is converted into a mindless assembly line divided against itself into nation-states and consequently producing no human progress.

Change versus progress

Reconsider the meaning of the word "progress". It has become synonymous with poorly-thought-out or deliberately destructive acts.

Activities producing dirty water, smoggy air, non-nourishing "food", and stressful noise do not improve human life.

This is not development or human progress.

Change is not necessarily progress. Progress worthy of the name means improvement. Therefore, a change isn't necessarily progress.

Pavement and asphalt are change. Potable water is an improvement.

A cell phone in every hand is change. Personal, flesh and bones face-to-face communication and understanding are improvements.

Conformity and comfort are threats to all contributions and advances toward human progress.

Buildings are blank walls representing blank minds, not progress.

Trade off

The nuclear threat is planned, and includes a high risk of massive fatal accidents.

The commercial threat is unplanned and a mindless, thoughtless march to certain oblivion.

The nuclear threat is well-documented & policed by critical observers. The commercial threat is not.

The commercial threat creates a constant state of deception, greed, tension, and war-without-arms, which has an occasional, but not infrequent outbreak of at least verbal violence.

Earth is not, by nature, a shopping centre.

In commerce, theft is institutionalized?

In true bank robbery, the bank is the perpetrator.

Users using used

Employment has taken more human lives than all of the wars, diseases, and accidents in human history.

Employment provides some lives with a stable routine and security. The same can be said for residing in a military camp or a prison cell.

Employers pay 80% of the world's employeed less than $300 per year. It's petty cash spending.

The employeed are on a changeless journey, without point of origin or destination. They're in the loop.

Employers sacrifice the afterlife for mere pre-afterlife fulfillment.

Publishers never get arrested for living off the avails of others' work, nor do many parasites called employers.

My writing could be essential reading for anyone who values life more than a job.

Employment is squandering precious days of life, but it takes an extra effort to try the unconventional, non-employment.

People are employeed to death. Employment provides the comfort of a padded coffin for humanity.

The scene around me at Tuglakabad is a statement about employment, corporations, and human life: Smokestacks belching toxic air surrounded by a huge favela.

The scene is describing human life as fodder for the factory furnaces, another form of Oswiecim consuming lifetimes over a long, laborious span.

Someone profits from this planetary and human destruction? Jobs, jobs, jobs... WIN-win?

The employeed are being shipped to their employers like oranges in a crate going to a banquet where they are on the menu.

It's a delivery system fuelling the life-gobbling cannibalism that we politely call employment.

Employment is a form of cannibalism. Employers consume lifetimes, devour employeed lives.

The employers eat living human flesh raw, like ikizukuri.

It is a long and torturous end for the employeed, stretching on for as many as 40 years.

Employing someone is taking out a contract on his/her life.

Why should I or anyone else sell a human lifetime for a house, a car, a pay cheque, and a pension?

I get up early because the day belongs to me, not to an employer.

Jobs are more important than life?

Ask the blacksmiths of yore; the fossil fuel company employeed; and the internal combustion engine assembly line employeed.

Computers can do the idiotic things we call jobs, while human beings are free to get to know each other better and to explore new worlds.

The ultimate conclusion of employment is to brainwash humans into believing that people are created by their own constructs instead of pursuing human work for human and planetary interests alone.

The employment-centred, material-wealth-only existence is abject human poverty. What unelected tyranny cannot boast the same results?

How many thinkers must give up their potentials, to become employeed or merchants, to live physically comfortably as inadequate compensation for a muffled, mute expression of their true lives and minds?

We are judged on being employeed consumers, not a self-sufficient and progressive lifeform.

The employeeds' only purpose is to support the employer's surplus.

I use employers for my ends, not theirs.

Good employers could give their employeed an extra week of paid vacation for volunteering while governments could declare that week of earnings exempt from income tax, if the time is spent volunteering.

A better educated or smarter boss is too much of a reminder of inequality. Feeling better than a boss is reassuring.

It emphasizes the wrongness of employeed systems. It shows the logical conclusion of systematized inequality.

It reinforces "trades" training only, a variety of education that's unsupported by broader, thought-provoking, reform-minded, action-stimulated education.

Jobs and skill replace democratic behaviour. Votes are cast for jobs, instead of for good self-government, self-improvement, and human progress.

Under the business elite group, most members of the citizenry are reduced to the same power status in relation to their elected government as they already experience routinely in their relations with the employers.

Government itself becomes an employeed of the business elite group. There is no longer a powerful advocate of the general interest.

The business elite is attempting a coup d'état of sorts.

As in any elite coup, the early objectives are to disable and seize control of the lines of communication normally open to the general electorate and its government, and to paralyze and destabilize the elected government, to try to force it to accept the unelected intruder's dictates.

If these initial goals are successful, the perpetrators need not take overt, visible control.

They can leave the elected government in place, to function as a puppet regime.

(See the news story about Bay Street businesses in Toronto jamming the Ontario provincial government's fax machines and blocking easy public access to the provincial parliament buildings in order to paralyze a government perceived as anti-business.)

The ruling purpose of business has never been to eliminate debts and make profits in order to contribute to the general welfare of the entire citizenry.

The main exception comes in the very basic sense of providing marginally subsistence income to the employeed, but only so that they can continue to function at a minimum level, to the point of being able to efficiently perform tasks which further the interests of only the employer elite.

This "investment in people" is not necessary when there is an adequate supply of replacement workers called "the unemployed", to prevent delays or halts in production due to sickness or death caused by poor working conditions, malnutrition, stress, and aging.

(About 40 years after I write these words, based on only personal logical reflection, a 60-year-old economics professor at a minor provincial university says the same thing to me about the employeed, as if it were a learned person's revelation.)

Balance sheet readers are the "self-made" people who send their children to university, while monetarily encouraging the employeed to tell their children to make money instead of studying and analyzing, which would eliminate the small employer elites' monopolies on real wealth, i.e. knowledge to fulfill their own lives and so flourish in living itself.

Cell phone gives a whole new meaning to the terms permanent employee and lifelong employment.

The sad fate of the employeed takes a turn for the worse.

Pensions never compensate the employeed who are discarded due to aging.

No amount of money or "comfort" is enough to compensate anyone for a lifetime of slavery and employment.

No one can possibly make up for the years lost entirely to serving and profiting only the greedy few.

In much the same sense as trying to make up for the atrocious treatment of concentration camp victims in Canada, USA, Germany, and Xiang Giang, after the maltreatment, the apologies and monetary sums offered to victims can never provide more than symbolic and moral compensation.

Perhaps I have never been fully aware of the truly revolutionary implications of my anti-employment thoughts.

They just seem to be logical, human behavioural objectives to me.

Yet reading about Lafcadio Hearn's book <u>Youma</u>, concerning the abolition of slavery in my current location, 144 years before the time of my current writing, I have pause for thought.

Even tyranny, it seems, has a comfortable familiar aspect to it.

Hearn writes that masters and people they enslave feel distress at losing their familiar, habitual, conventional roles, even though it's liberation for the people enslaved.

Unfortunately, Hearn's writing also reflects his European era's racist paternalism toward all non-Europeans.

But his writing also helps to explain why the employeed are trapped and remain in the trap of employment, the Sisyphus standard issue existence.

In employment, the tasks and products are increasingly distant from direct action in support of human life and human progress.

Employment societies trivialize life, humanity, and family by trading a life for mere monetary gain and material possessions.

Employment-centric society is truly the most primitive and only marginally survival-subsistence society. It retards human progress.

No wonder the skills, works, and lives of ancient humans impress me so much in museums. They are misnomered pre-history.

Employment-centric societies are non-history.

Generations of lost skills, talents, and genius are caused by training people to serve others by subservience, employment, and sacrifice, rather than serving others by doing what one likes, i.e. does best and so contributes to improving all human life.

The best way to help others is by setting the example of doing what interests us most.

That means something we prefer to eating and sleeping; something that makes us want to work on it from the first moment of daylight until fatigue hits in the evening; something that makes us forget clocks, calendars, and makes us use every living moment with energy and vigour; something that makes words such as holidays, office hours, and retirement so obsolete that they are meaningless.

Employers spend the Cold War bribing the employeed with the illusions of security and employment.

Thereafter, employers dump both because of rumours of the death of government rule.

Employers merely want higher profits, while only grudgingly granting the employeed lower salaries, fewer benefits, and more layoffs and closings.

When the insecurity age arrives, employers frighten the employeed into accepting security and employment.

The fear among the employeed means returning employers to a ruling position closer to the age of Jacob Marley and his partner Ebeneezer Scrooge.

Not having employment could make life seem precarious for some people. But just being alive is dangerous.

There are no safe places or secure times. Trying to hide from the world and oneself in employment is futile and self-deluding. It is suicidal behaviour.

Walking too fast across Odori Koen, I find myself in a play area, slowed down by gravel. The annoyance of being slowed down by the rough surface passes quickly.

More places should be gravel to slow us down, to make all of us always late, so that we can take our time instead of selling it to employment.

Pensions are calculated according to years of service to employers, not according to the accomplishments of productive human lives.

Employers have a history of using the employeed's marital status and number of children to force the employeed to comply with company demands and to trap employees into debt, dependency, and security fear behaviours serving only the employers.

Employers exhaust the employeed to the point of inducing them into idleness and mindless behaviours during off-the-job "free" time.

Low or no activity, non-productive jobs leave the employeed effectively out of work and unable to behave actively or productively in a positive sense, in even the non-job settings.

The elite are the most disadvantaged and handicapped group in the world.

Unfortunately, the elite are the only such group with the power to impose unpleasant experiences on the bulk of humanity in their daily lives, through elite ignorance and contrivance, eg. inflation.

The profit motive seems to be a game where everyone loses.

Employers induce an era of grasping instead of seeking, an era of inactivity instead of thought and actions. It is stagnation.

Money makes employers and employeed greedy and insecure simultaneously.

I prefer to make less money, spend less money, and have larger, longer, deeper experiences in distant places.

Thus the employeed existence has no allure for me, no spell to hold me back from a full life.

The right to support and to improve our own life and the world around us, instead being a mere tool for an employer, is the best right to work.

Futures universe

"The future" implies there is only one outcome whether it is based on predestination or choice.

In reality there are futures, a variety of alternate outcomes based on a number of possible choices.

Every lifetime has the potential for more than one future.

Futures, like the universe in which they take place, are always characterized by uncertainty.

Spontaneous choices, coincidences, and hap-hazard events turn out to be the rule rather than the exception in determining futures.

Each moment that we act consciously the futures change, not just at the end of our journey. Every action and thought alters what happens next.

Not knowing the futures makes them better. There's always something undiscovered to look forward to encountering and using as a source of learning.

You don't have to worry about the futures if you are making the futures. Apparently, you cannot make history, just interpret it while making the futures.

Futures come from humanity, not from present distortions of humanity.

If the futures never come for anyone, the concept of "future generations" is sheer abstraction, theory, and escapism conjured up by people losing all hope and giving up trying to improve life now.

Their legacy is only despair, promising only one future that repeats the past over and over again, for all generations to come.

Leaving the futures to some abstract, vague, unknown concept such as "future generations" provides the managers of the status quo with unchallenged power to do anything, including nothing at all.

There is no "future generation". It's up to us, now.

We can boldly go in search of many different futures.

We can try new technologies. We can try less rigid forms of social organization to eradicate barriers between human beings.

Or, we can merely cling to the long-gone past and illusion-based security of the present.

But, the moment that we let our artifacts, constructs, technologies, etc. rule and control us, that is our time of death as an intelligent species.

Having to think for myself, to make my own path, and to leave much baggage behind, means totally uncertain, unpredictable futures. It's wonderful!

The status quo constricts the circulation of life, breeds unchanging behaviour, based on a superiority complex versus one's forebears, and a fear of the unpredictable future possibilities.

The status quo avoids unpredictable futures by fighting them back until they become over-whelming.

The cultural future(s) of Nippon might be decided by a cartoon studio.

The futures depend on us all living on a planetary scale, at least until we have more than one home planet.

Futures are changing so rapidly that even the most famous science-fiction writers can't keep up with them.

The futures of human life depend on non-urban expanses.

The futures of all humanity depend on us pre-venting interveners, meddlers, manipulators, and self-declared aiders from harming any more humans and human civilizations.

In the past they have done more bad than good.

The crusaders, conquistadors, inquisitions, missionaries, residential schools, etc. were all supposed to have good intentions.

But too many have been founded in prejudices and have reeked havoc on all humanity.

It's our responsibility to repair and prevent further damages in the present and futures that are caused by the projection of thoughtless and destructive behaviours and precedents that were set in the past, in error.

I ask the question of futures very profoundly, not just socially or in a narrow perspective which calls upon me to feather my own nest or, as I would express it, pad my own cell in this madhouse society.

The ability to spend more money does not create better futures.

The USNASA shows that the futures belong to those who can do more with less.

The "third" world is already masterful in this effort.

Eighty per cent of humanity is maintained for a fraction of the costs per person of the "first" world minority.

Apparently, a "first" world model of 'the future', built upon the deification of material wealth, creates poverty in many senses, including superiority complexes and IMF loan sharking.

While changing the futures of many people, the perpetrators of the European colonial-national era and its inheritors have had a great deal of difficulty in differentiating between human progress and destructive behaviours.

Conservatives and conventionalists are people without their own true futures of active free choice.

They will never know their true selves and never know what they truly want to do.

They are people put in moulds from birth.

We need to move toward the futures, not get caught up in European era sophistry and follies of defining nationalities and dividing humans.

That sophistry just enables the greedy and privileged to retain their undeserved status and power, while most people in the world struggle to survive.

The European colonial-national era occupation, extended under another name in Martinique, only prepares dominated people to forget their roots and pretend to be Europeans.

Such a future without a past has no value. Better to rediscover one's realities than lose them.

Martinique's "Ville Morte" general strike is closing down the greedy money economy and cutting the circulation of polluting cars. It's not a bad future.

Why vote for anyone who says s/he can't do anything to improve life now, but can only act in some future paradise?

A person who really thinks about the possible futures shows the depth and breadth of his/her thoughts by always becoming and remaining flexible and adaptable, instead of getting stuck in one, single path or pattern for a lifetime.

Regardless of ideologies, philosophies, ways of life, nation-states, societies, cultures, etc. and all the other theories, desires, and routines we follow in our daily lives, the prime concern uniting all humanity is our survival instinct based on self-interest and self-preservation as a species.

If we lose our survival instincts, and do not act in our own interest to support life, the same interest of all living things, we are only ensuring that we will lose our entire life support system on this planet.

If we lose life-support, we will exclude all potential futures and be left with only one possible future-species extinction.

Unlike spawning fish, our futures making work is lifelong, not just the moment of fabricating our replacements, the new people who start from zero, i.e. the real primitives called children.

Both before and after their birth, we can change the futures by every move that we make while jumping along.

The best way for us to help our fellow humans is to thoroughly scrutinize, strictly analyze, and tightly regulate all of those people and projects that are called missionaries, development groups, and the like.

We may not be able to help the past, but we can right the present and futures, by applying what we learn from past errors.

We should not carry on from the rotten roots of past errors.

We must plant better roots to reflect our informed and more liberal present knowledge and learning.

Building upon, carrying on with the past's evil heritage, only makes us a party to it.

At first, it's good to see their familiar faces, a former favourite professor and an elder former fellow student.

But as they sit across their desks from me, they begin rocking in their deadly routines, moving their bodies in a creaky, rhythmical, unchanging pattern.

Their faces take on the pall and glumness of spooky characters in horror movies in their rigid swivel chairs. The stare at me gravely.

I think they're about to try to take possession of my soul. I'm right.

Each says, in identical tones and programmed words, "Have you thought about the future?" The emphasis is exactly the same, on the word "the".

They see only one future, more of the same mind-dulling intoxicants: comfort, routine, security.

The "c" "r" "s" make a "CRS!" sound, reminding me of some utterance of invading aliens in the Donald Sutherland version of the "Invasion of the Body Snatchers" movie.

Fortunately, the rocking old men before me don't rock hypnotically and put me to sleep.

They're living on cruise control, cruising in place in automatic pilot.

They drift off in the clouds, unaware that their path is actually in a thick fog surrounded by mountains.

A thinker should not pose a question that s/he is not willing or able to try to answer him/herself.

(Postscript: My former fellow student tells me, years later, that he quits his job as a dean at a trades college, saying he should have done so years earlier. He starts an international consulting service.

My former favourite prof, living into his eighties, finds that his "future" excludes communicating with his former employer and with me. He fades to blank?)

A CBC-TV news reader says that he picks up a Canadian astronaut who is hitch-hiking in Florida.

The astronaut is making space travel more economical and strengthening contact between the general populace and the still elite space travellers?

A news reporter from the U.S. finds a former space project scientist selling ice cream at a shop. Outreach? A space future beyond reach?

The image of future times that H.G. Wells des-cribes in his book, <u>The Time Machine</u>, is a world in which the always slaving "third" worlders end up eating the always playing "first" worlders?

At present, the always playing "first" worlders are devouring the lives of the always slaving "third" worlders.

The futures are unforeseeable. That's what makes life interesting.

I could not want to visit a fortune teller. That would spoil all the surprises, discoveries, and fun.

In going to the futures, all of the interesting parts are getting there.

"A secure future" means pretending all is stagnant, and making it so.

Time's passed

If any recorded history or associated historio-
graphy actually resembles times past and des-
cribes events accurately, it's remarkable.

The last word in history is the writing of whoever
lives the longest and succeeds in hiding, rewriting,
and reinterpreting other writers and story-tellers.

There is no objective history of anyone, any time,
or any place still existing or no longer existing. It's
all a matter of perspective and opinion, not objective and inalterable fact.

Superior Force

The widely discussed "superior force" in human life may have its roots in the initial biological experiences of people.

We are tiny at birth. Our first life experiences are dependencies on hospital workers and parental care.

So the workers and infant's parents become part of all later desires and loves for a good, "superior force", such as:

"mother earth", "the fathers" of confederation, "the greatest nation on earth", "the great powers", "big brother", "our father, who art in heaven", etc.

They can "keep us safe" and "take care of us" in injurious and fatal ways.

Monarchical dictatorships spread the myth and illusion that their origins are divine, i.e. coming from a divine "superior force".

Some Canadians still treat the inheritors of that psychological indoctrination legacy with such awe, deference, and reverence that it is difficult for a non-believer to hold back laughter.

In this context, the idea of an unelected senate sitting over the elected parliament in Canada is not so strange, considering that the head of state is an unelected foreigner.

The U.K. and other nation-states embracing sub-servience to home-grown monarchies with so much enthusiasm are the truest of all believers.

Monarchs are put on such a high pedestal, accen-tuating their remoteness in every other way from most people, that monarchs might just as well be heads of the world. Terrestrial gods need jobs too?

Since monarch Louis Bourbon dismisses Canada as a few hectares of snow, without ever seeing the country, I don't have to see the inside of Versailles to dismiss it as a few stuffy rooms full of old mir-rors and decaying furniture.

So I just walk through the garden, to its farthest point from the palace. Fresh air is great.

Truly Friendly

Better to pursue human relationships that are liberating, not asphyxiating.

A friendship is rare and special, not common and superficial.

Friendship means more than mere coincidence of birth, socio-economics, employment, geographic proximity, etc. Those are simply commonalities.

Friendship exists in flesh and blood, live and in person, in a touching of hands, in a reading of facial expressions and body gestures.

Friendship is nowhere near a mutual isolation in distance, opinions expressed in anonymity, barren typed words, or flat, lifeless two-dimensional screen images of some paperless pen pals.

I reject the anglophone habit of saying that someone is "just a friend".

But just friends are much better than unjust ones.

Anyone using the term "just friends" is down-grading and diminishing the value and importance of his/her relationship with another person.

Anyone using the term "just friends" is under-rating and demeaning the most significant, intimate, profound, and wonderful of all human relations.

Friendship is not something to switch on and off like the "friend" and "unfriend" buttons of anti-social media platforms with their anonymous, artificial, superficial, scatterbrain, butterfly approach to human relationships.

Friendship is a relationship not requiring a license, a certificate, a ceremony, monogamy, a public pledge to lifelong adherence, all strictly governed by government and religionist rules, regulations, and absolute laws.

Friendship doesn't require such window-dressing, formality, official certification, and absolute religionist adherence, "until death do you part".

Friendship is far superior to marriage.

Friendship is open. It can expand to many people.

Friendships can end without going to divorce court, government bureaucracies, and religionist approval.

In great contrast, marriage is closed and discourages friendship, except, ironically among heterosexuals, same-sex friendship.

There is no reasonable excuse for thus making marriage isolationist and leaving its adherents lonely for friendships that are not same-sex.

Do same-sex marriages have similar limitations, restricting friendships to non-same-sex friends?

For the unmarried and for some of the more fortunate among the married, friendship is open to all and unlimited to just a few, even if few or many qualify by their expression of true friendship.

A good friend is someone you feel so familiar with and so relaxed with that you can fall asleep with him/her.

In friendship, cooperation and mutual confidence are essential.

Otherwise the friendship is at risk, actions are at cross-purposes and counterproductive. Extra dangers can arise.

A friend is someone you can live with, without feeling any "obligations".

You are not acting out of a sense of duty or loyalty.

You are not following a convention that strictly defines friendship, with a fixed set of rules, regulations, or laws.

You are not preoccupied with some negative, social, or customary politesse when dealing with a friend.

Friendship is not about simply winning or repaying favours.

Friendly behaviour is not some kind of ledger sheet.

You act in the other's interest simply because it feels good to each of you.

If someone rejects me because of my cloths, hair style, or spaces between my teeth, then they are surely not worth my interest or friendship.

A friendship, once begun, does not require constant or frequent contact or physical presence.

Absence and proximity don't absolutely maintain or destroy friendship.

A weaker friendship is more likely to suffer due to proximity rather than due to absence. People can find out that they are not friends after all.

A true friendship does not prevent a friend from living a life apart from a friend.

Adventures, explorations, and discoveries made outside a friendship can eventually profoundly enrich each friend.

I probably have fewer than 10 friends, which I consider a huge number, considering the tough way that I define friend.

A person should not feel obliged to do, say, or think what "everyone" does, says, or thinks just because one doesn't want to offend friends and softer people who are unanimous or thoughtless in the deep sense.

If not informed, friends and softer people can host and spread the malady of ignorance just as surely as the carriers of any disease who aren't aware that they are infected and have great potential to spread the contagion.

True friends don't demand conformity, compliance, or monolithic behaviour from friends.

Friends don't question, criticize, and mock nonconvential behaviours among friends.

Friends accept each other's reality and don't try to convert or change a friend according to someone else's judgement and standards.

That's a vital condition of friendship.

When this condition is not met in my teens, I'm quiet. In my twenties I'm polite.

I'm also annoyed by the unfriendly people who don't give me the same respect as convention-bound people who let societies and others decide their lives for them.

I make my own personal choices and decisions. I write my own guidebook to my life. My true friend understands and respects these facts of my life.

But in my thirties, when someone asks me to explain why I don't just fall in line for caffeine, nicotine, alcohol, or Kool Aid, I speak out.

I say: Your question needs analysis, not my behaviour and personal choices.

What kind of society do you represent that questions differences instead of questioning conventions; that questions innovation and invention instead of questioning conformity and blind following; that questions thought instead of questioning unthoughtful mimicry?

Is this the question pattern on the road to a "free", "democratic", and "pluralistic" society?

In personal behaviour, do we question only diversity, but not question the status quo?

A person who tells me how to behave or present myself would be better advised to get a job as an image consultant for some egomaniac.

But s/he need not apply to become my friend.

A person who tries to manipulate or dictate my thoughts, behaviours, or aspirations is just a meddler to me, not a friend and not even a helper.

I tend to be attracted most to people who do not waste their energies trying to be accepted, to "fit in", to conform, to be "respectable", to gain "status", "fame", and monetary "wealth".

Life is too short for such loser games.

Couplings

The people you know the longest can be the ones you know the least.

The most generous people can often be the ones you know the least and who have the least material wealth to share.

You know only their humanity.

A marriage licence is merely another way of imposing bureaucratic control over human behaviour.

Marriage too often fits like a necktie, a symbolic collar to bind and inhibit both parties to this formalistic coupling.

Marriage is an illusion built upon an illusion.

If male-female couples are formed mainly due to natural human reproductive species survival instincts, that must mean that only same sex couples experience true love.

I am the product of a mixed marriage. My parents are male and female.

What does that make me? Bisexual, transsexual?

There's a big difference between loving your neighbours and falling in love with them. Both are loving relationships and therefore good? Or love is bad?

Behind every great woman there is an insecure male supremacist trying to hold her back and take credit for her accomplishments.

Even a good person who becomes a husband may "have and hold" back a woman. He's following his standard issue existence, Sysiphus conditioning.

How about same sex couples? Who holds who and does either one hold back the other?

As my married friend Ely, and mother of three says, "If another person causes a couple to break up it means the couple are already broken."

V.D. stands for Valentine's Day. STD is a vehicle that's something beyond the LTD model?

Motherhood/Fatherhood Issues

Motherism is inegalitarian and anti-democratic.

a. Dictatorship rules the roost

The "Little Red Hen" story is used to shame people into helping others. That's how my mom uses it.

In fact, however, the hen is an anti-democratic model.

The hen is an autocratic dictator who unilaterally decides the entire future agenda and appoints herself boss.

She expects unwavering adherence to the goals that she alone sets. She expects loyal participation in the methods that she alone chooses.

She attempts to elicit obedience to her unilateral master plan by asking everyone in her realm to participate in the achievement of her goals.

As she arrives at each of her unilaterally-decided steps along her unilaterally decided path to reach her unilaterally decided goals she says, "Who will help me..."

Predictably, since everyone else is completely ex-cluded from the entire goal-setting and planning process, no one shows any interest.

So, in the end the dictator hen retaliates by deriding and punishing everyone for not partici-pating, i.e. not fulfilling her wishes.

Her retaliation against and punishment of others is to reserve all the benefits of her master plan to herself.

She can rationalize this dictatorial and greedy be-haviour by mouthing off self-apologist phrases such as:

"The people are ignorant." "The people are apathetic." and "The people get the government they deserve."

No wonder nobody wants to be a part of anything that the hen does.

This story also reveals why male supremacists con-tinue to plague the world and why so many women are still trapped in domestic servitude.

It is a failure to teach both males and females how to become full and equal partners and participants in planning and running the world and in seeking alternate behaviours to the stereotypical and domestic servitude routines and models of existence.

Moral: Gender unilateralism, often fuelled by impatience and blind ignorance of potential, can only reinforce both female servitude and male supremacy.

The Little Red Hen is both a ruling dictator and a victim of self-imposed slavery.

Incompetent males are a consequence of con-ditioned behaviour.

Parents teach boys to believe that "making yourself at home" means doing nothing. Only girls can grow up to be "home makers", after boys grow up to be "home builders".

Males who reluctantly and begrudgingly share "women's work" are feeling an emotional reaction and attitude which more women already feel but fail to challenge instead of sharing their misery behaviour with male partners.

As the old U.S TV commercial puts it, "If I don't do it, who will?" a frustrated woman say.

b. Returning Son

My dad tells a story of a son who constantly declares his father stupid until finally, after the son goes around the world, the son returns to his father and is amazed by how much the father learns during his son's absence.

Apparently my dad believes that people hearing this tale are supposed to conclude that real world experience helps younger people to better appreciate the knowledge coming from the experience of their elders.

However, I add a new part to this instructive tale.

My variation of the story is that the father is very disappointed to find out that after going around the world to places he doesn't know and after having experiences that he never has himself, his son only learns what father already knows, nothing new and nothing more.

There is no advance from one generation to the next.

Family Values more or less

My family is all living things.

A personal family is comprised entirely of the people you choose to live with, regardless of biological links, immediate or not.

Otherwise coupling could only be incestuous.

In human history, as opposed to nation-state history, family would mean the people you live and move with, people who work together for mutual benefit, to promote movement, not slow it down.

"Blood relatives" would be an unimportant alien concept, unknown and probably unknowable, aside from the maternal line. (This is long before DNA testing.)

The only important blood links would be with the entire human species. All for one and one for all.

In this way, neither the biologically older nor younger are ripe for nation-states' manipulations and controls serving the nation-states' ends alone.

The conversion of family to a restricted, narrow, and limited biological concept defined by different family names alone is a very divisive concept.

It amounts to causing an unjustified and potentially adversarial divisive schism in humanity.

It supports a honey-coated dictatorship, wherein no one dare do anything innovative or original because it might disrupt "the family".

In this context, family means nothing but a nation-state surrogate.

Urbanity

Wind tunnels and heat islands are urban centres' contributions to inhuman engineering and inhuman geography.

These unnatural new formations of sorts are making urbanization an ever more inappropriate form of habitat and an obstacle to planetary evolution, impeding the ability of life forms to survive, flourish, and progress.

Urban centres are monuments to architects, urban planners, and other people with even bigger egos and delusions of grandeur.

Humans become conditioned and air conditioned.

In cities, humans are so fully isolated from their traditional contact with natural dangers that they find it necessary to fill the gap, as their contribution to nature, by developing new dangers such as economics, crime, and pollution.

Instead of the bird calls and animal sounds of our natural habitat, major urban and suburban shopping buildings provide only unnatural noises.

We lose touch with our abilities to hear songs, mating calls, warnings, and invitations.

Unnatural noise confuses the human senses and prevents awareness, concentration, and comparison.

The objective seems to be to disorient shoppers, block their thinking abilities, and prevent them from making rational, reasoned decisions.

For the seller this means creating good customers, i.e. people who bring money and spend it without hesitation or reflection.

But the in-store experience must be terrible for the sales clerks.

Like alcohol drug servers who work every hour of every night in a Singapura disco, constantly bombarded with over-amplified sound, employeed minds must turn to mush.

The only order in such abused and paralyzed minds can be the order given and followed. Maybe it's a commercial adaptation and refinement of military training.

Shopping increasingly becomes the ultimate spectator sport.

We go through the doors and the cash register ticket wickets to just take what's available at the price shown, and hand over payment.

It is as mindless, impersonal, and non-participational as the self-hypnosis of watching television or staring at a more recent blue screen, the old and new training machines for shoppers; a consumer act simulator.

PADD, personal advertising delivery devices going by various names, and almost glued to shoppers now crossed eyes all the time, make TV look as innocuous, trite, and amateurish as the abbreviation of television.

The folly of urbanizing humans is clear. Neither we nor this planet are designed to function optimally in conditions of scarcity.

Market economies are a symptom of induced incompetence and laziness.

How unfortunate we are to live in cities, where everything living and real is paved over.

How can a city or town be a living place if the main goal of urbanism is to eradicate a natural setting and pave it over to prevent life from thriving and reasserting itself?

According to an NHK documentary about northern Canada, many Inuit choose "primitive" plenty over urbanization's "advanced" poverty and scarcity.

Even the tourist industry may soon have to deal with the reality that people will not pay thousands in foreign currency to shop in expensive places with bad air, where the local way of life has been eradicated by urbanization.

Might as well stay home.

From afar, Bhaktapur's horizon gives me the impression that I'm seeing an ancient predecessor of the modern high-rise skyline, but in brick.

Inside the town, I note the absence of trees and plants. Life is bricked over here in the past, just as modern suburbs pave over life now.

The urbanizing choices offered in some places are either a sterile urban centre or a filthy urban centre.

These are two forms of the same deprivation, the same poverty for human life.

In neither case are humans able to know life and experience natural surroundings and equilibriums.

Whether slowly asphyxiated and sterilized or always grimy, human life is limited.

While Xiang Giang is held by a European imperial regime, the urban centre is a dusty, noisy construction site that's never quite ready for human habitation, sitting in the middle of a crumbling, high-rise slum.

Any setting which prevents people from fully expressing their human qualities is unlivable.

An urban area is best defined as a rural area's septic tank.

Suburban subdivisions are twisted reality, coiled like dangerous poisonous snakes. Human life is mortally threatened.

Urban and southern residents of Canada might be fearful and/or traumatized by Canada's seemingly endless area of uninhabited wild lands.

Southern Canadians may call these rich lands of dense forest growth teaming with life "uninhabitable" only because there are no big cities in the trees.

The only value that urbanites see in wild land is fuel to burn and other resources to put an end to the wilds.

Wild lands are also places to render "tamed" for fantasy escapism by way of polluting motor vehicle.

196

The cities of Canada and elsewhere are surrounded by the real Earth that they attempt to hide and eradicate under dead pavement, metal, glass, and concrete.

Thus, it is the urban centre which is actually uninhabitable.

Since when is a big city the ideal environment for human life, or any other life?

Try sleeping on concrete and finding something edible growing in an urban core.

Conservative economics really are costly. They are not about conserving anything worth conserving, such as life on Earth.

What some people save in spending and deficits in public finance, they end up paying out in house security systems, dirtier and more dangerous urban centres, the fully unpleasant realities of homeless street people, unbreathable air, etc.

In a small town, a suburban shopping centre kills off downtown and replaces chatting pedestrians with parking lots and fast-passing cars on major roads.

The sterility and anonymity of the out of town shopping centre makes us all strangers, even in very small towns.

Why not enliven the middle, instead of voiding it?

What point is there to levelling and paving over natural, fertile, rural land, instead of recycling already disturbed, paved, and ruined midtown spaces?

The initial land costs of suburbia may be cheaper, but the mounting social costs of eliminating the established centres of community are mounting to become enormous.

Anti-human urbanism, commercialism, and industrialism are the real ideologies, not bogus Euro-centric theories such as capitalism-communism polarity.

Urbanism, commercialism, and industrialism are the three real ideologies. They are part of caretaker-society making, which means acculturating all of us out of our humanity.

A Europe-type modern urban setting designed to prolong elite rule over humanity is a hard place for a Terrian or any other free-thinking human to flourish.

Snow is a means of solving urbanity.

Snow crystals cover even the worst gashes of urbanization and all its refuse, showing us how it all need not be so.

Noise waves are all but stopped, yet human voices and pleasant sounds travel farther than on a snow-less day.

Instead of a constant roaring, vehicle noise can only groan far off in the distance and struggle in desperation against insurmountable, well-padded and deep pocketed banks of snow.

Only night ploughs can howl in the sleeping hours of central Toronto and Quebec City.

Snow liberates melodic sound waves. Whispers and songs are enhanced to carry farther than urban anti-noise bylaws permit.

We can hear each other speaking softly together when no urban din blocks the waves of friendly voices.

The softest sounds massage our usually pained ear canals, long irritated by the drone of routine.

Robotic daily urban motions are paralyzed by snow, allowing the graceful strides and full expression of our suddenly liberated selves, if we choose.

Graceful, slow motions replace the urban humdrum's daily, frantic death throes of human inner remains.

In Djakarta, a friendly, raised eyebrow, and a spreading mouth are lights in the urban darkness.

In a city, the sign "park" has come to mean only a concrete area for polluting motor vehicles.

Australia is alien urbanization transplanted from afar to cover and conceal a wild land of climate extremes and natural phenomenon.

The lively favela patterns in Brasil, Nippon, Han-goo, and Chuang Hwa lure me in to explore.

But I would normally make deliberate efforts to avoid and stay out of the sterile, lifeless movie back lots called suburban subdivisions.

People confined to subdivisions use their cars to communicate most of the time, coming directly out of their garages into the streets, using remote control devices to close the garage doors.

So there is little probability of human contact, even among neighbours who pull out of their garage co-cocoons simultaneously.

A smirk and nod become the warmest and most profound forms of human contact on a typical day in suburbia.

The favela demands intelligence, ingenuity and improvisation, i.e. thinking and action for the residents' survival.

Passive dwellers of suburban grid locked cages require only a driver's license and road signs.

The urban has set and fixed limits.

Nation-state capitals and other planned cities are constructed to limit, divide, and reduce humanity.

Urban and suburban represent the imposition of isolated dwelling places separating humans from each other in boxes and artificially patterned routes all leading nowhere but to employment and shopping, instead of uniting humanity around itself.

Natural versus National

Homeland is in reality no more than land with water and air, not artificial barriers of nation-states.

National isn't the same as human. In the nation-state, the problems of Earth and nature are kept apart from the nature of humans.

The problems' source is the non-nature of constructs and artifacts which take on pseudo-lives of their own.

Humanity and nature are one and the same. The nation-state is our Frankenstein's monster, but not composed of anything that actually ever lives.

We are in a situation much like the sorcerer's apprentice in the classic animated film "Fantasia". The nation-state is the broom and bucket drowning us.

Only together can we humans become the sorcerer to stop the unnatural flood.

This is the age of disenlightenment, of overcertainty, of insecure over-security, of the artificial over the life-form.

Nationalism is nihilism. During my parents' youth, tens of millions of people die in only six years for the perverse concept of nationalism.

Nationality is merely conditioned behaviour, programming. It is not natural or hereditary in any way.

Nationality is but an adjective, not a noun. Nationalized people are like tinned peaches.

They are peaches, not tin. We are people, not nationality.

So national labels needs to be modified, to more clearly distinguish the packaging from the human content.

It is we who must adapt and adopt, instead of trying to reduce or eliminate natural conditions which challenge and exercise our intelligence and adaptability skills.

One Inuit recounts that the ice fields of the north have always been a "paradise". Inuit cannot understand why other people ask, "How can you live there."

I am puzzled by people who leave the human habitat long ago, and whose descendants thereafter start to make it uninhabitable, to force out and exterminate those who chose to stay, by polluting and paving our common ancestral home. Global concerns and the problems of the non-elite and minority cultures are too minor to distract the separatist elite from its holy cause of creating a new nation-state for all to admire, at any cost.

Humans are not the objects or subjects of a nation-state. They are its antithesis.

Nationalism is ignorance of the entire human community, its overwhelmingly obvious commonalities, and the world around us all.

Nationalism is a form of dictatorship under which the human good, the planet's good, and the good of all natural forms of life are subjugated in favour of "national interest", "national security", and "nationality".

The nation-state is constantly portrayed as more important than life.

Killing humans is all right for the nation-state. Polluting the natural environment is all right for the nation-state. The nation-state is inanimate.

Maybe trees survive not by being complicated in the manufactured, synthetic sense, but by being naturally complex.

Are paintings of natural scenes just a legitimate excuse for idly looking at nature, without being accused of laziness or of wasting time?

In Nippon, people gaze at the spring sakura and autumn leaves the way that people in Canada gaze at autumn leaves.

Nation-statism masqueradism

Opponents of global human identity, unity, and progress come in many shapes and sizes.

Among the most evident are those who are called separatists and who call themselves by a monarchical dictatorship term, sovereignists.

Sovereignty has become the latest code word for separatism because it can be made to sound nebulous, innocuous, and inoffensive to most people who don't know the origin of the word.

Sovereignist comes from the monarchical dictatorship term sovereign, meaning monarch.

It is ironic when used in Canada, since "sovereignists" declare themselves anti-monarchist.

It's bizarre when they declare themselves "independentist", a term more often associated with opponents of European colonial-nationalism and, in the Canadian context, implying that Canada is a colonial power and its provinces are colonies, not voluntary members of a federal system.

Of course only Newfoundland and Labrador and Nunavut join Canada after holding referendums. The other provinces and territories never vote to become part of Canada.

Bélanger-Campeau's report on Canada's future is not a report at all, but a concert of discord. Keith Spicer rewrites it, many years later.

Separatists pursue the mythical ideal of the inevitable success, beauty, and panacea of a new nation-state to further carve up humanity.

Nation-states only carve geographically first, working on the human bodily mutilations and murders later, by international war.

Provincialists are separatist-nationalists by another name.

They invent and emphasize artificial, superficial, geographical, and stereotypical differences among humans to divide us, to turn us against ourselves in a permanent intra-human civil war, and to impose restrictive constructs over us to alienate us from our natural selves and to generally dehumanize us all.

In security

If our primary objective is mere security, then we cannot hope to produce, motivate, and retain the inquisitive, thoughtful adventurers and risk-takers who are essential to a flourishing, fully prospering human species.

They are essential to a sustaining lifeform.

People who live long enough to become weak and helpless dependents must sometimes dream, with deep regret, that they don't have a full life when they're younger and stronger.

These older people must finally, but all too late, realize that they miss having full lives, and all because when they're younger they want to "make sure" they'll be "secure" when they become older.

But weakness and helplessness in old age becomes deadly security.

Their younger selves only "make sure" that they can finally be secure in the knowledge that, as elderly people, they no longer have a chance to try to have a fulfilling life.

Youth and health are worth more than all the supposedly "precious" metals and "prized possessions" in the universe.

Youth and health give us more strength, liberty,
and choice than any other "valuables".

So why trade them or sell them to the highest
bidder employer?

We can horde and stash away "valuables", such as
"savings", but we can't store and retrieve youth
and health in old age.

Today's "security" rules, laws, and technology
would make all the dictators of the past envious
and will make all present and future dictatorships
much more powerful and difficult to remove.

The "first" world is always and endlessly pursuing
an elusive and unattainable illusion called security,
to secure a position of dominance over everything
and everyone forever.

A military dictatorship is devoted to securing and maintaining its rule. Imagine the contents of time capsules buried by military dictatorships.

Military headquarters is an asylum for the criminally insane. It plans to kill. First degree murder is intentional.

Castle ruins, armour, and gowns only tell monarchical dictatorship rulers' stories.

Security means the supremacy of rules, but...

Rules aren't written to be broken or obeyed. Rules are essentially reactions to extreme and rare case scenarios.

Life and rules are mutually exclusive domains.

Living isn't a matter of following rules. Following rules isn't living. It's only going through the motions by a guidebook of rules.

Living is about natural survival instincts which keep us alive and help us to flourish. Security cannot and does not do that.

Expending youth

My dad tells me to prune trees by cutting off the new growth branches so that the old growth branches can grow stronger.

I reply that this approach, applied to humans, would mean killing all the younger people so that older people can prosper.

Later I realize that this is the rationale for war.

We cut off the lives of the younger people so that older ones can have wartime and post-war "economic booms".

Youth is the first to go. Youths are the first to go.

I don't worry about negative futures such as aging into fragility and weakness.

Aging is a force natural to Earth, a force that I can only retard with a healthy lifestyle, not eliminate altogether.

Gravity and atmosphere age and kill us, if a bad lifestyle and stress don't strike first.

Seventeen and eighteen year olds from India work in Punta Arenas, send their rupee pay home, and survive on only board and stipend.

A military dictatorship in Argentina sends seventeen and eighteen year olds as canon fodder for the U.K. professional military to slaughter in the war of Las Malvinas.

When the young are slain, their elders are supposed to become so angry that they lose their senses and rush to vengeance by supporting war and sending more young people to die.

JFK's murder is a later-day symbol of the kind of young minds which are blown apart by the nation-states in crimes against humanity, such as the 1930s/40s wars.

War is a way we can treat each other as people.

But there are many more positive ways for people to treat each other to save young lives instead of repeatedly squandering them.

Gang violence

Military government is a glossy, shiny, and almost flattering term for criminal rule.

Gangsters, military dictators, and terrorists are products of inequality and obstructions to equality. So equality is only gained by violence?

The "developed" "first" worlders are like a street gang meeting someone who wants to be a member.

After trying very hard to prove that s/he is just like the gang, no matter how many painful initiation tests s/he passes, the gang leader can tell him/her that s/he doesn't have what it takes to become a gang member.

The fact that s/he is just as good as a gang member is an unvalued fact. S/he has to be called an official gang member to feel worthwhile.

If "developed" or "first" worlder were objective and positive terms, based on observable good human behaviour, then who would merit the title and what would it mean?

Mind colonizing

The European colonial-national era's most appalling legacy has been to make the culturally rich, multi-civilization majority of humans believe and behave as if they were inferior to the European minority.

It's an incredible historical manipulation which should fascinate future historians.

Majority plays by minority rules. All previous history and life is abandoned to suit Europe's dictates.

The European colonial-national era is no age of inquiry & discovery.

It's an era of Inquisitions, Conquistadors, and Crusaders.

It's a time when there's no place in the world for non-European perspectives, historiographies, or civilizations.

The consequences of the European colonial-national era type of world view include plagues, decay, deterioration, destruction, and genocide.

The European colonial-national era Inquisition mentality:

If unfamiliar behaviours and newly-acquired knowledge don't fit previous assumptions, learning, and established conventions, then they must be wrong.

What the churchist missionary schools (residential schools) try to do by one means in Canada, until very recent years; the U.K. occupation regime does in Singapore; bogus language schools try to do in Nippon; and the "first" world tourist industry does in Thailand.

In polite colonial terms, it's called assimilation or integration in a negative sense.

The goal is acculturation, assaulting humanity based on Euro-U.S. predatory superiority complexes and concepts of unicultural, unilingual primacy.

One world language and culture aren't decided by freedom of choice or referendum. They're imposed by force, business, and techno-invasion.

As a young U.K. employeed at a Barcelona language business establishment says to me, English language teaching "is the last vestige of colonialism".

Anglophones' agents try to colonize the world linguistically so that anglophones can romp around the world proclaiming that "English is the world language".

Stay with the anglophone tour group so that no one can cast doubt upon your linguistic faith.

Development

Development is so relative. European monarchical dictators of times past consider Canada an undeveloped and unattractive domain.

For France, Canada is a permanently frozen asset.

For the U.K., Canada is a remote military post and fur trading camp inhabited by French-speaking colonists and undesirable locals.

The southern Americas follow Canada as recipients of abuse, equated with cheap fruit, rubber, wood, and wool instead of expensive beaver pelts.

The epithet this time is "banana republic", i.e. nation-states ripe for political destabilization by two empires, U.S.A. and C.C.C.P., like the U.K. and France during the U.S. civil war.

The futuristic city of Brasilia and stately European architecture of Rio de Janeiro, Santiago, and Buenos Aires (often called "the Paris of the south") are insufficient to gain the "first" world "developed" title.

But not being "developed" isn't all bad.

221

People who don't live like the "first" worlders do are living proof of the fact that "first" world ways are neither essential nor superior.

In the transitional, high transience years of an era, or a lifetime, when an established order is becoming unable to impose its will effectively, the non-"developed" have an increasing advantage and more potential.

What a shame when anyone can only see the world through "developed" windows.

Perseverance, survival, and human advancement under the most severe conditions provide the ultimate evidence of development, adaptability.

The mere accumulation of material wealth and an increase in comfort are lesser and misleading signs of development.

We want a better world, not merely a materially comfortable one for a few or for many. We want human life to flourish, not to decline.

Shallow participation, with little need for thought, effort, courage, risk, or commitment is always in style in the "first" world.

The visible evidence of poor nutrition, poor hygiene, poor health, and poor English usage among anglophones is overly apparent to even the passing observer in the U.S.

So many people look psychologically unhappy and worried.   The obesity and ignorant miscommunication are appalling.

Yet the U.S. is not an atypical "first" world area.

For these lives, what is the difference between modern living and digging bugs out of stumps?

What quality of life?   What standard of living? What low use of intelligence!

Structures and leaderships fail to build a mass of regenerating, growing humans.   Only they would be living testimony of an era making a positive difference.

Otherwise humans only continue to endure a succession of rise and decline empires, the rises and dips of "economic cycles".

Why not instead enjoy a rising humanity, connecting times with awareness and knowledge of the past, present, and future, in daily life and in every lifeform?

There's a big difference between daily awareness of just the same old familiar narrow, temporal-spacial routes, such as employeed standard issue existence routines, versus a daily, broad awareness that the routines are no more than disjointed jerking motions with no positive impact on or significance for the drab condition of a rather small lifeform, on a tiny grain in the universe.

It's the difference between surviving another day and creating alternate futures.

A Shinkansen in Canada would require Canadians to think about positive futures and to work together for solutions instead of blaming each other for every problem in existence.

That would be a huge development.

Canada has less than 1% of the world population and more than 40% of the world fresh water supply. Time for redistribution is long overdue.

"First" worlders call themselves "the developed world".

"First" world rule: To succeed means to become a "first" world lookalike, to become foreign to oneself.

The U.S. and S.U. non-identical twins have less than 10% of the world population & interfere with the lives of the other 90+%.

The "first" "developed" world is not the Earthly paradise it pretends to be or that desperate migrants imagine it to be due to "first" world propaganda about itself.

How could the tiny "first" world minority work so little for so much of Earth's wealth?

The "third" world needs a big population to feed the appetites of the "first".

The struggling "third" world youth who live in the streets could learn to stop slaving for the greedy ends of "we, the developed", the parasites on their backs.

Without "us" holding "them" back, "third" world youth would be enabled to far exceed the competent, participating years of we "first" worlders.

In the "first" world, plenty vs. poverty becomes an objective, not just a theory of condition.

What has the "first" world contributed to Earth and its lifeforms aside from pollution, obesity, and tens of millions of war deaths over a 60+ year period?

The "developed" waste lives, time, etc.

No wonder we have to go abroad to "third" world areas, to buy beautifully-crafted souvenirs.

They are souvenirs of a heritage which the "first" "developed" world loses at home and tries very hard to destroy abroad.

It is time to recognize that there is just one world. There is no "first" "developed" world with a divine right to impose its minority rule will.

In Toronto and in the southern Americas, I learn about differences in what people consider problems and what they debate.

In the "first" "developed" world, the topics are abstractions, such as housing and inflation, not practical living realities and not the basics of human life such as where to sleep tonight and how to get something to eat to stay alive another day.

The "first" "developed" world puts form ahead of substance. It's as if Marshal McLuhan were describing the "first" "developed" world, not just communications theory.

The "first" "developed" world is so artificial that it will go down in history as the first biologically-fed synthetic.

"Developed" countries seem to have foregone democracy, opting instead for mediocrity. This can be fatal.

Military dictatorships thrive on our "first" "developed" world ignorance and support.

We don't see what our companies and governments do elsewhere in order to maintain our "first" "developed" special status, our distinct societies.

If we do not unravel this mess soon, our victims well become our masters.

We must abandon our greed, careers, 9-to-5-ism, real estate, etc., instead of our co-human partners.

Our equal partnership is the only thing that we have to offer them.

Let's be remembered for more than a few crumbling buildings, some broken dishes and vases, and the old stumbling crackpots leading us on to our own demise.

Competent people are conscripted out of their own lives and into the "first" "developed" world. This drives them out of their minds.

In "first" "developed" world "travel", the emphasis is on minimal effort, minimal contact, and minimal learning.

That's why there's minimal or no positive impact on education, foreign policies, and election voting "back home".

My message for First Nations trying to integrate or feign integration into the European-Occupation "first" "developed" world "white man's society": Why bother?

Non-First Nations people can gain much by discarding their superiority complex and "first" "developed" world myths, then critically observing and analyzing other humans who have contributed so much more than the European colonial-national era to human survival and fruition.

The only common enemy of the "first" "developed" world is any effort to end the unfair trade-debt dictatorship and the artificially preserved comforts and privileges of the "first" "developed" world minority rulers.

Major "developed" world's impact:

Formerly healthy villagers become choking, water-less pedestrians in a fabricated environment which produces only holes in the ozone layer protecting earth lifeforms and a "green house effect" destabilizing the delicate balance of climates and temperatures which support life as we know it on Earth.

After the general conclusions that I reach about "first" versus "third" world relations through my own observations and logical deduction, I'm not as surprised as I might have been to learn that 80% of "first" world aid projects fail and that's an im-provement from the previous 97% failure rate.

Evidently, missionary aid projects remain the same as they are historically, contributing nothing to humanity.

They are little more than acculturation and destruction schemes, eroding locally rooted mores and replacing them with alien mores that are not rooted in local experience and therefore only superficial.

Projects without local roots cannot grow or succeed in the long run.

Most foreign aid projects fail due to lack of research along with "first" worlders' incompetence and superiority complexes.

Only recently have aid groups begun to consider the value of involving locals in the planning of projects, according to a course that I take at l'Université Laval.

Excluding people from their own "development" is like social housing and welfare projects in Canada and favelado forced relocation projects in Brasil.

These projects and relocations fail because they're planned in isolation from the recipients' influence and control, then simply paid for and imposed by government and its private corporate partners..

This is the most worthless of gift-giving. It contributes nothing to the democratic behaviour or improvement of the needy or humanity as a whole.

In this gift-giving, it's the lack of thought that counts.

"First" world run aid projects, by their very nature, are unlikely to succeed.

For the "locals", the "first" world aid worker appears to be monetarily wealthy, like tourists, and s/he has a privileged visible minority status.

The appearance raises expectations which block communication and perceptions generally. Or it becomes a rerun of European colonial office rule.

The non-local ("first" world) aid worker is perceived as an incompetent with lots of money, like a guided tourist.

S/he has to depend on locals because s/he cannot even perform basic cooking and washing chores.

S/he is also more than likely an illiterate deaf mute in the languages of the "third" world.

Luckily for him/her, s/he has money to pay for locals to take care of him/her. S/he is the only true aid project recipient?

The locals become a pool of cheap labour servants for the "aid" workers.

The aid projects thus help the locals by providing them with low-paying domestic, chauffeur, and translation jobs.

As I write in Brasil, it would be better for "first" worlders wanting to help the non-elite "third" worlders to send me their cheques, instead of contributing to formal "first" world aid agencies.

Even with my relative ignorance, I could do a lot more community development work to help non-elite locals than ten times more money in official grants to "first" world aid agency workers.

The only obstacles to giving are that I'm not government-sanctioned and tax-deductible?

South Africa's former nasty apartheid minority dictatorship is a microcosm of the "developed" "first" world minority who rule over the majority of humanity through the apartheid of immigration and economic policies.

Mere visitor's visas to Canada cost more than a minimum salary in many "third" world nation-states.

Few "third" world people can "qualify" to immigrate to the "developed" "first" world.

Immigrants are screened by socially isolated, higher income bureaucrats with university degrees.

These bureaucrats have no expertise in critically evaluating qualifications in any field, including their own.

Are immigration policies the result of learning the tragic story of what happened to most of the world when European colonial-national era "colonists" and other invaders solemnly believed that they

234

were free to maraud around the planet, to loot, pillage, despoil, and acculturate without asking permission to enter lands beyond Europe and without applying for visas to go abroad?

It is time to end planetary apartheid while "first" world minority rulers still have the power to do so voluntarily.

I have to learn much more about why the "third" world majority are more competent and more developed than the "first" worlders.

Could I help the "first" world with the knowledge that I acquire?

But who in the "first" world is willing to listen to and to learn what the "third" world has to teach?

A previous "first" world ignored and mocked Marco Polo for his accounts of the Great Khan of the Mongols.

The "first" world of today is still trapping itself behind the superiority complex curtain.

My lifestyle is at least ten years ahead of my "first" world born contemporaries.

When the "first" world's fragile walls tumble, the mobile will be the best prepared to carry on.

Today's <20% of the human population "first" worlders believe themselves to be the best masters of the world, deserving every billion IMF dollars that they collect from the "third".

If we of the "first" world can see the insidious influence of 500 years of European colonial-national era history, we can overcome its negativity, greed, and self-destructive behaviours, to help ourselves to rediscover ourselves and to become fully human.

We can become non-dominant partners, like spouses who treat each other as equals, in a humanity enriched by full expression of the true selves of all humans everywhere, unimpeded by fear of mere survival against the onslaught of the greedy.

Each person can use him/herself to her/his full potential, to compete with him/herself, toward a goal of personal excellence that inspires and advances us all, instead of mindless conquest, which merely limits and ultimately crushes the pursuit of excellence, and retards all human advancement.

The domineering see nothing to gain from the open and free expression of all humanity.

I'm glad to be able to see human cultures, variety, and creativity before they're all wiped out by concrete, metal, glass, and asphalt.

Today's religionist structures, i.e. the banks and their commercial/office/luxury hotel/condominium towers, could remain as evidence of our era's elite centrism, just as the epicentre dome in Hiroshima is evidence that war is also anti-human.

If you don't act as the "first" world does, and expects everyone else to act, you are not developed.

It is not a new theory. It is a theory which frequently blocks humanity in times past too.

Throughout recent history, at least, anything different from accepted behaviour and concepts is considered wrong or inappropriate, by definition.

Love of the inanimate makes people forget the animate, i.e. that life is more than a collection of possessions and money.

People in caretaker society countries, i.e. "developed" areas are programmed to pay anything for anything, including expending their entire prime years of life for nothing.

If you don't want to pay, the merchants just shrug and hold the goods for the 99% of customers who pay like zombies.

"First" place last

"First" worlders show the absolute folly of being led instead of thinking.

Since most of "first" worlders believe that "we" can only live as "we" currently do because we have the best way of life:

1) "our" first reaction is to reject all change that doesn't reinforce "our" way of life;

2) "we" presume that all other people must want to adopt "our" way of life because it is the best, i.e. "we" know what is best for "them";
and
3) until "they" succeed in completely copying "us", we can only help."them" by sending food and other things, since "we" understand that "they" must be inferior because "they" live differently and "they" are so slow at becoming "us", and so "they" come to depend on what "we" do for "them".

"Their" failure to be "us" is all their fault, not ours.

Our greedy, wasteful, polluting materialistic life-styles and way of life can't be wrong.   Our definition of progress and our use of technology can't be wrong.

This "first" world illusion of "superiority" is very unlikely to salvage, revive, or save the "first" world from itself.

I realize that I should not expect breakthroughs. Ignorance is a convention in the "first" world.

When we do <u>not</u> know the "aliens", be they in Toronto or in the "third" world, (such as Rio de Janeiro, Córdoba, Valparaíso, etc.), we can mistakenly accept our experience of the "first" world around us as typical of the universal norms of behaviour.

Therefore, we can mistakenly assume that if we are discontent, it must be due to our lack of adherence to "first" world conventions.

We suffer entirely because of our non-conformism, our looking beyond the immediate "first" world setting to learn something not already known by everyone around us in the "first" world.

We're preposterously unconventional!

We can conclude that only in the "first" world can we know all that we need to know to be content.

So, it is better to learn only and exactly what "we" know, instead of trying to learn something more from anyone or anything alien to the "first" world.

The "first" world mentality:

Those who have the ability to act positively remain inert.

The best example of a nasty minority and closed society is the "first" world.

It rules by dividing the human majority against itself, perpetuating the myth that the majority is a minority.

Democratic processes and the opening of societies are being retarded and impoverished by the double-edged sword of aging, materially-wealthy populations in the "first" world and their closed doors to non-elite in migration.

"First" worlders consider human problems non-existent and unusual anomalies in their own lands, but typical and normal everywhere else.

Today's "first" world is like the reputed state of the ancient middle land, Chuang Hwa, when the elite there reportedly felt that the outside world was inferior, had no lessons to teach, and had nothing worth seeking.

Considering the primitive state of Europe when Chuang Hwa was a central world civilization, perhaps the elite of Chuang Hwa were correct.

But in that context, I would probably disagree.

There is much to learn beyond the self-declared centres. There are people, places, and wonders that equal and surpass every era's "first" world.

Not knowing or recognizing that reality is a perilous and fatal folly. That's clear in the freezing deaths at Champlain's Port Royal.

Only the non-European knowledge of how to survive a very severe winter could save the Europeans. The First Nations "savages" taught them.

The first step toward a better world is for the "third" world to educate and evaluate the "first".

The "third" can set up training camps, providing "third" world teachers and information aid packages to train the "first" how to live in their own habitat, where they are now rendered incompetent, mindless, and impotent by employment and routine.

Then the "third" world could decide whether or not the "first" world could play a useful, positive, and active contributing role as partners of the "third" world majority of humanity.

Maladies

A sick society expresses its illness in different ways. When I'm in my teens it's overt, violent prejudice.

In my thirties, I observe the sick society from a distance, while I'm mainly in the southern Americas and Nippon.

The sick society manifests itself in greed and materialism. I see it in the guise of the IMF and World Bank loan sharks.

Now the sick "first" world society reveals itself in its renewed self-delusion of a neo-European-colonial-national-like era.

I hear a television commentator saying, "There will always be a third world."

So the 80% are destined to live under the minority rule of the 20%?

The commentator goes on to say that the 80% don't seem to have the diseases of the 20% because the "third" world has poor statistics.

So we can forget about "first" world scientific researches who appear in the news saying that our diseases, such as breast, stomach, and lung cancer are a product of our "first" world society?

Why do we assume that we can cure our sick society by pretending it's not sick and by pretending that others aren't healthier due entirely to their poor statistics?

We are out of touch with reality. That's our most prevalent fatal illness.

Dependencies versus Accomplishments

I see the world of routines personally and through the stories of people trapped in lifelong routines. Routines are a self-reinforcing addiction.

Many people come to see the calm monotony of routine as an end in itself, and misinterpret the vacant looks and social smiles as happiness.

Maybe it's like working on an assembly line and being satisfied to see boxes of fully-assembled products at the end of each day.

Or, it's like construction workers who can see how many square metres of buildings they build and can show it off to others.

"See that building. I built it!" they say with proud looks and gleeful pride.

Writing can be the same way. See this page. I write it!

But the type of writing that I produce demands more than looks, smiles, pride, and brawn.

Anyone can write, but few try. It's much more interesting and stimulating than routine. Writing is more strenuous, tiring, and challenging too.

Writing makes me much happier than any lifeless routines ever could.

Writing can happen anytime, anywhere, and unexpectedly, almost like photography and all inspirations.

We all need something in life that makes us think, reflect, and change for the better.

Writing keeps me alert and observant. It gives me a deep sense of accomplishment.

Nobody tells me when, where, what, how, or why to write, or who to write about. I make up my own mind, in a profound sense.

Planetary Human Life support

Smokestacks and exhaust pipes are cannon and bazooka barrels pointed straight at our life-centre heart- the air, water, and land which keep us alive.

If Seoul and Barcelona can blame former dictators for air pollution, then Los Angeles must just be very stupid for electing and supporting political representatives who accept increasingly poisoned air for a very long time.

Discovery

The most significant discovery that we can make is the discovery our own ignorance.

From that starting point, we can explore what we don't know, always remaining aware that we are learning what others may already know.

Unfortunately, in times of yore, the isolated residents of the European peninsular backwoods west of Asia delude themselves into religiously believing that they're going where no one has gone before when they land on shores unknown to them, but already inhabited by non-Europeans for millennia.

Such is the origin of the nonsensical claim of "discovering the new world".

Non-Eurocentric books describe the arrival of Asians and Vikings in the "new world" long before Europe's self-congratulatory "age of discovery".

Also, since African empires are closer to southern parts of the "new world" than is Europe, it is probable that Africans too arrive in the "new world" before Europeans.

Some of the descendants of our common African ancestors are the darker-faced people who greet Europeans in what the latter rename "New Holland"?

Humans have a long history of migrating and living across the sea and land of Earth, long predating the European "age of discovery".

Eurocentric historians ignore long-term global human history, supplanting and distorting it with a European colonial-national version of history.

What they call history is the official version of events approved by the monarchical dictatorships and the religionist "first estate" of Europe.

They send missionaries and military forces around the world to destroy and erase all non-European civilizations, governments, religionisms, and history, following in the tradition of Rome erasing Carthage from world maps.

Eurocentric historians embrace this type of imposed ignorance and transform it into widely-accepted, conventional truism lauded in school text books.

A mentality of accepting myths as truths, for whatever purpose, is no basis for discovery, learning, accurate observation, or rationally determining desirable futures.

Will our explorations and discoveries beyond Earth be subjected to such calculated manipulation and amnesia by indoctrination?

Solar flares of a super nova could melt all of our history too, so long as we sit motionless in the aura of only one star.

Divergence & Discordance

Ideological conflicts are merely superficial covers over real conflicts of programmed interests.

It's about putting labels on contrary perspectives of the same reality.

It's calling a natural variety of perspectives "conflict" instead of complement.

It's seeing differences as negative instead of positively healthy and thought-provoking.

In the polar regions of the planet, the east-west distances between people become increasingly small.

Abstractions

Did Locke, Smith, Marx, or the others of their eras and before, ever live in countries beyond the European peninsula and mid-latitude Americas?

Do they make careful and detailed studies of Bharat, Persia, or Chuang Hwa, the homes of the most ancient human civilizations, before writing "world" theoretical models?

Otherwise, how could they gain sufficient knowledge to make "universal" generalizations about human beings, histories, and societies?

In fact none of the above-mentioned "world" theorists leave Europe before writing their theories about "the world".

Only Marx, long after publishing his "world" theories, leaves Europe once.

During his last decade of life he goes to a spa in Algeria to try to find a cure for an ailment.

Thus Locke, Smith, and Marx, along with many other European "experts" on the "whole" world, follow the European tradition of ignorance displayed by Colon and others.

Their writings are occident-centric, steeped in European colonial-national era self-delusion, self-aggrandizement, arrogance, and myth.

Ideologists spend their time writing unintelligible manifestos in dingy libraries and other isolated settings, describing cures for the ills of parts of the world where they have never been and know nothing about.

More the pity that "third" world students should be encouraged to extend European era control over their minds, by taking the cloistered European philosophers' views back home to replant them in alien soil.

Marx is gone, but Locke step and Keynes disease continue to disorder human living, undermining human knowledge and being.

In seeking the disappearance of government "interference", the business elite group is showing itself to be a proponent of the disappearance of the state which would warm the hearts of Marxists everywhere.

Conventions need people to survive, but people don't need conventions to survive. Likewise all ideologies.

Creative Opposition

Creative opposition to any system is a desirable necessity.

The true role of opposition is to replace the system, not to replace others in the chairs of government.

If, on the contrary, a position of influence and formal power is gained, maintaining power becomes prime.

The work of creative opposition to the stagnant reality of any status quo is discarded.

Formal power and every status quo are intertwined and interdependent. Criticism and change are outside both.

I know little of Bharat, but in Mahatma Gandhi's work there is an example of a first step in creative opposition. He never seeks or holds office.

The next step, after removing the U.K.'s European colonial-national era rule, is to replace the U.K.'s colonial power structures, including the U.K.-type parliament.

Gandhi's campaign to end the U.K. occupation of Bharat includes creating a form of participatory public action which can also be the basis of the people governing themselves rather than using surrogates.

Yet the surrogates and U.K.-type parliament remain, long after Gandhi.

Had he not been assassinated before his participatory model prevailed...?

Defaming

Who wants fame? It comes with stress and unhappiness, according to biographies of the famous.

If you are famous, there are people who you never meet who will love or hate you for no reason except for total ignorance of you as a person.

Others who you do meet, sometimes people you don't want to meet, are in your life only because fame obliges you to spend time with them.

Thus fame puts you at odds with total strangers and acquaintances you don't seek out.

Fame destroys what little freedom you may have as a nobody.

Canadians think almost nothing of themselves or those who make important historic contributions to Canada.

A multitude of roads and buildings are named for the heirs and successors of European monarchical dictatorships and other people with no roots in Canada.

In contrast, the smallest towns in Argentina and Chile, two nation-states much smaller than Canada, always seem to have a Plaza San Martin for San Martin de los Andes.

Argentina's municipalities always seem to immortalize Belgrano.

Louis Riel, the only "father of confederation" who founds two of Canada's eventual ten provinces and the only "father of confederation" to be executed by the Government of Canada, is only recognized in the two provinces that he founds.

Caring & sharing

Better we should plan Canada's future by soliciting the participation of the rest of humanity as equal partners, rather than drifting along to oblivion or making futile and greedy attempts to keep 99.5% of humanity out of Canada.

What we do not plan to share will just be taken out of our hands.

The same applies to the European peninsula of Asia and Austral Asia.

Descendants of Canadians who live in the homelands of the First Nations over the centuries will come to know how the First Nations feel when frustrated potential immigrants lose patience and start openly and aggressively invading, instead of trying to enter casually as "settlers".

It's called poetic justice.

The billions of people living outside of the "first" world could well decide that a truly democratic world cannot allow a minority to put up barriers to the migration wishes of a majority of humanity.

(Update: 200 million climate change refugees are on their way, looking for new homes.)

A 70% majority of Euro-South-Africans vote in favour of ending a nasty apartheid minority dictatorship and establishing a democratic system there.

In some ways, these voters are unique in history. They are perhaps the first people to vote for a better world future.

If they can vote for majority rule, surely the rest of the "first" world minority rulers can do the same.

Instead of making immigration part of ministries that can make it part of building a better future, the U.S. government is combining immigration with the federal police and spy agency, to secure borders, i.e. just to keep people out.

This is six years before successful attacks on the U.S. military and financial centres.

Democratic Architecture

The grandeur of Paratini is well worth the visit. Huge paintings and mirrors celebrate the state government.

No wonder people and politicians have illusions about the greatness of indirect government, i.e. rule by surrogates instead of citizens.

Representative government distorts democracy by building and keeping such palaces for itself.

Although the seat of the U.S. government is built by a child, L'Enfant, it impresses and perhaps intimidates all but the most destructive and ob-noxious vandals.

Yet this deceptive construct, an architectural mu-seum of styles taken from defunct European empires, reassembled around an Islamic dome, precedes and goes far beyond the more recent façades of Las Vegas (U.S.A.) casinos.

Both the capital and the casino locations create illusions that millions are willing to shell out for-tunes to prop up and to almost devote their lives to perpetuating.

Canada's palaces, the federal and provincial parliament buildings, are the heritage of all-powerful European autocrats, monarchical dictatorships.

None of the above are the architecture of democracy.

What is the architecture of democracy?

It's not palatial. It's not the engineered towns, such as the northern hemisphere's isolated and lifeless subdivisions.

Nor is the architecture of democracy rows of identical, equidistant boxes labelled houses and apartment buildings.

The architecture of democracy is spontaneous, adaptable, portable, temporary, and expendable.

Mongol tents, First Nations teepees and wigwams, transient miners gold rush camps, and evolving favelas are the archetypes of the architecture of democracy.

Favelas

Favelas attract me because they express intimacy and personality. They don't come out of an architectural journal. They come out of actual lives.

What does a favela represent to people who don't know it?

To the church-builder, it's a place to talk about some unearthly paradise in a life after death.

That's because the provision of poor public services in favelas by government/corporate bureaucracy have to be accepted in life.

A favela is a place to make people read "holy" books, pray, and accept less, on the grounds that a superior being wants it that way.

Making the source of poverty look divine is an anti-deity religion.

For some architects, a favela is a place to destroy and replace with an expert-architect-dictatorship concept of housing and streets.

For charitable donors, a favela is a place to send money, food, clothing, or medicine all the time

because the residents are considered and assum-
ed to be incompetent and incapable of learning,
taking action, and improving their own lives.

This is a "benevolent" and soft form of arrogance
derived from a superiority complex.

All of the above are truly foreign aid, entirely alien
to favelas, to favelados/as, and to their realities.

For many others not admiring favelas from afar, a
favela is a place to ignore and to forget most of
the time.

When the ignoring ignorant are reminded of a
favela's existence, it is redefined as a "problem" to
be left to "experts" or "do-gooders" because "it
really has nothing to do with me".

As Dickens' Scrooge would say, "There are
organizations and agencies to deal with "those
people" who have "economic problems".

Aims, Fears, & Ways

I seek to go beyond risk-taking. I'm going for more than mere fame, money, and prestige. I seek to make and direct my own life.

People who are expected to fulfill other people's expectations, anticipations, and desires already have a great obstacle to fulfilling their own lives.

I'm an ambitious person, too ambitious to be restricted by any adherence to convention.

Convention is an illusion used as a tool of exploitation by those who see it for what it is, mindless routine.

I need to act with courage and determination in non-conventional ways. I won't rot as a social captive or exploit others.

Wherever I go I want to say, "I come here to observe and to learn, not to rule you, not to judge you, not to manipulate you, not to buy you, not to own you, and particularly not to make you into me."

I go places to learn, not to impose the diet of my paternal homeland, not to create tourist bubble ghettos, and not to confirm stereotypes, prejudices, and misinformation.

I am not out to help entrench conventional "wisdom".

I am not a tourist on Earth.

All tourists can be a menace, whether moneyed or sloppy. They impose their pretensions, foreignness, and superiority complexes.

In contrast, I try to behave mild-mannered, humble, unobtrusive, polite, and unassuming outside of Canada. It comes naturally to me.

I do not act surprised if something is different from my previous experiences, only intrigued, curious, and interested in learning.

I am not presumptuous or anticipatory. I do not impose my expectations.

So locals everywhere can find me human, likeable, friendly, and sometimes quite curious compared with the tourist hordes.

Locals can smile and greet me as a visiting neighbour, instead of a "foreigner".

No matter where I go, I almost never have the sensation of being a "foreigner" because I'm not alien to humans or to this planet.

I try to be conscious of my every facial expression: friendly, inquisitive, serious, or neutral unreadable, depending on the context when I am a guest.

Although I am a vigilant critic of the IMF, and a severe critic of materialistic "wonderland" comfort naïveté, etc., I think it's unfounded to feel guilty simply because I'm not living in poverty, sick, hungry, or dying.

If this type of guilt were valid, one should logically decide to eliminate the guilt by embracing poverty, getting sick, going hungry, and dying.

That would produce absolute equality while eliminating more human life instead of helping anyone.

Far less extreme action usually soothes the guilty feelings of people who normally live at the expense of the people who are supposedly being helped.

But realism calls for learning, for self-directed adult education which enables people to identify their own problems, to design their own solutions, and to work to implement them through their own actions.

That's not found in a gift wrapped package from people far away who are desperate to deal with their guilt, while carrying on as usual in their daily lives.

In Bharat, I look around at the healthy, well-fed, well-dressed-looking locals and see no beggars chasing after them.

Instead, the beggars are relentlessly pursuing the sloppy visitors carrying backsacs.

Local elites are known as people who don't give, don't care, and don't offer any help to their unmoneyed neighbours?

Here I can feel no embarrassment about not giving what little I have.

My lifestyle is so simple that I have no inclination toward any sense of guilt for living at the expense of others' discomfort or disadvantage. I don't.

I cure my "first" world childhood greed. My lifestyle is now quite harmless.

I don't travel to exploit others or to entrench the tourist industry plague.

You can't make a prophet or profit in your own country because it's too easy and familiar there. You have to go outside for inspiration and motivation.

You can't be Superman on Krypton.

It's not that I'm completely fearless. I have a fear too.

I don't wish to be lying in a hospital bed at age 100, wondering why I don't do more, why I don't go further when I'm younger and can do so.

This expresses not only my fear, but also my spirit and my goal in this pitifully short human lifetime.

That's why my youth is not a function of some uncaring employer who sees my life as something to purchase and use for eleven months or more months out of twelve until I'm worn out.

That's why my youth is not merely a list of numbers in a) a mortgage ledger, a gauge of death, or b) a car and appliance payments ledger; and not c) merely a name of a parent on a record of live birth.

Parents' self-imposed sacrifice, of giving up deciding their own futures, becomes the parents' licence to cajole their children into also sacrificing their right to decide their own futures.

A lifetime needs to be more than role playing.

I would sooner starve to death at 60 years old than be used when I'm less than half that age. I feel this way from at least the age of 26.

But only in my thirties do I gain the courage to act upon my own wishes.

I choose more difficult routes than necessary sometimes.

I don't regret not having seniority or extended annual vacation time granted to me by an employer.

I use my life instead of permitting others to use it.

All I am trying to do is use my own brain to make my own life, nothing more – nothing less.

I'm simply trying to make what I consider to be the best use of my knowledge and experience in the highly precarious existence which a human being has on a hostile planet.

Perhaps it's impossible to be alive without doing harm.

We don't all wear face masks and gently brush the path before us, to make sure that we don't inadvertantly kill any insects, as my dad observes some religionists doing in Bharat or Bangladesh.

A person who expends too much effort considering only the harm or hurt that every thought or action could involve is obsessed with negative thinking and might end up spending an entire lifetime as a servant of all around.

This person is no longer alive. All hurt and harm is done to this person instead of to others.

Sovereign

The only real sovereignty worth pursuing is human sovereignty, within the global planetary world.

Nationalism attempts to destroy human sovereignty, by turning humanity against itself.

Nationalism is a negative form of amoeba, constantly dividing against itself in an unconscious attempted suicide.

Barriers to human sovereignty:

1) a person not trying to do what s/he wants to do;

2) distractions and diversions taking away the person's attention from his/her central interests;

3) other persons discouraging him/her;

4) others directing or manipulating her/him.

Human self image

In Rio de Janeiro, I'm astonished not to see a mulatto face looking back at me from the mirror.

In Fukuoka, I'm expecting to see an eastern Asian face looking back at me in the mirror.

I perceive myself as a human being just like all the people around me.

Being a "foreigner" is a deranged state of mind.

I wonder why anyone can be singled out for internment and concentration camps anywhere.

What profound reason could ever justify such evil treatment?

"They" were born.

The camps are racism training centres run by racism.

The elites see themselves differently, i.e. as elite.

Who would remember the ruling elites if their corpses were not insulated from reality in both life and death?

We really do not know how long we can stay anywhere or in life itself.

The homeland is the land itself.

Who is more primitive, past or present people?

Past people don't have the "advanced civilization" threatening human species survival and life as we know it on Earth.

With so many new archaeological digs and unknown gaps in our past, how can human history ever be written?

We need to eradicate the "race" myth, personally. This is a call for action, one-to-one, not abstractions or anti-discrimination laws alone.

We have to live together as the same humans.

Concluding Cites

This need not be an era of merely constructing various forms of autocracy based on an economic dictatorship of neo-monarchist-dictator oligarchs.

People living under democratic-like systems are failing to use their power for all people.

I don't mean the "charity" of bossing others around. I mean listening very carefully, observing, and then asking how you might be helpful, if at all.

If we, the few privileged, who call ourselves "first" worlders and who prioritize most of the people in the world well below ourselves, devote as much energy to living as humans as we do to our shopping temples, we would consequently be doing wonders for everyone.

We would no longer be pretending to be innocents and "victims of them", saying "Why do they hate us."

Fortunately they don't or we'd all be dead by now.

We would no longer be passing most of our waking somnambulant time playing with toys between periods of being hard-working employeed.

We would no longer be sleeping in air conditioning, driving around in polluting vehicles, and voting for people devoted to making the world worse for everyone except us, and saying, "We're having unusual weather now. I wonder what's causing it."

We "the developed" will go down in history as "the ones who could have made the world better for all, but didn't bother to do so".

We "the developed" will go down in history as "the ones who relegated humanity to a side event, a hollow public service announcement".

VOLUMES FROM MYTHBREAKER

Terrian Journals series:
A Sketch of Terrian History
Terrian Journals' How To Make The Nation
Terrian Journals' 500 Years In Louis Bourbon's Few Hectares
Full Employment: Not Fulfilling
Terrian
Caretaker Society
Terrian Journals: Living as a Newcomer
Middle Earth Journals
Re discovery Journals
Fukurokuju No Kasumi Journals
Sabbatical Journals
Departure Journals
Adventuredate Unknown Journals
Away Team Journals
Searching For South Journals
Inonakanokawazu Journals
КАЗАНЬ Journals
Exile Journals
Tenjin Journals
Next Journals
Terrian Journals for the Misguided
Terrian Journals' N.S.R.: Not Spying, …Really!
TJ JNG: Terrian Journals' Jokes Nobody Gets
Terrian Journals' Half Serious
Terrian Journals' Disbelief
Terrian Journals' House Trap
Terrian Journals' Virtually Camping
Terrian Journals' Crystal
Virtually Dead
Terrian Journals' Maximum Insecurity
Terrian Journals' Mandarinas
It's News To Me
Terrian Journals First Anthology
Terrian Journals Second Anthology
Terrian Journals' Issuing Citations

Pre-Terrian Journals:
Explorations Of Inner & Outer Space
Out of Context
Terrian Journals Origins

Archway series:
Archway: Six Year Book of Dreams
Archway: Lifetime Rhyme
Archway: Life Before Dreams
Archway's Valentine Love
Archway's Garden Rhymes
Archway's Christmas New Years Rhymes

Additional Titles:
Language Learning Secrets
Trying To Teach Languages In The L.B.E. World
An Adult Book About Education
Terrian Journals' Miss Schooling?

Fiction: Terrian Journals' Political Science Fiction

www.ingramcontent.com/pod-product-compliance
Lightning Source LLC
LaVergne TN
LVHW052017080426
835513LV00018B/2059